STDs

STDs

WHAT YOU DON'T KNOW CAN HURT YOU

DIANE YANCEY

Twenty-First Century Medical Library
Twenty-First Century Books
Brookfield, Connecticut

Illustrations by Anne Canevari Green

Published by Twenty-First Century Books
A Division of The Millbrook Press, Inc.
2 Old New Milford Road
Brookfield, Connecticut 06804
www.millbrookpress.com

Library of Congress Cataloging-in-Publication Data
Yancey, Diane.
STDs : what you don't know can hurt you / Diane Yancey.
p. cm. — (Twenty-first century medical library)
Includes bibliographical references and index.
Summary: Explains different types of sexually transmitted diseases,
how they are contracted, their symptoms, and treatment.
ISBN 0-7613-1957-3 (lib. bdg.)
Sexually transmitted diseases—Juvenile literature. [1. Sexually trans-
mitted diseases. 2. Diseases.] I. Title. II. Series.
RC200.25 .Y36 2002 616.95'1—dc21
2001027793

CONTENTS

STDs

UP CLOSE AND PERSONAL

As most teenagers will testify, relationships are a top priority in the bustle and hubbub of modern life. The world would seem lonely and meaningless without friends to talk to, rely on, and love. But relationships, especially those involving the opposite sex, can be complicated, too. The emotions and feelings that arise while falling in and out of love can sometimes be bewildering and difficult to sort out.

Sexual feelings are extremely strong when two people fall in love. Many couples, however, have not thought about their own sexual values and limits before beginning a relationship. Caught up in their feelings for one another, they don't worry about whether their actions are going to make them feel guilty or remorseful later. In the rush to experience sexual intimacy, they spare little thought for whether they are risking pregnancy, illness, or even death—and then it is sometimes too late.

The difficulties experienced by the teens in this book illustrate what happens when inadequate planning, poor judgment, or the thoughtlessness of others leads to health problems. These young people are coping with sexually transmitted diseases (STDs), bacterial or viral infections that can be passed from person to person during intimate sexual contact. Their names and the details of their lives have been changed because of the personal nature of the diseases. That does not make each person's mental and physical distress any less real. All have had to face the fact that STDs can affect anyone and everyone. Most are now reconsidering the actions that led them to contract an STD and are hoping to avoid making similar mistakes in the future.

NAKEESHA AND SERGIO, SEVENTEEN YEARS OLD

Nakeesha and Sergio are seventeen, plan to be married, and have a one-year-old daughter, Alicia. Three months ago, Nakeesha discovered that she was pregnant again.

Recently, Nakeesha woke up with a dull pain in her lower abdomen. The pain didn't go away. Sometimes she felt like she might have a fever. After a few days, she went to a doctor, who diagnosed her problem as *pelvic inflammatory disease* (PID), an infection often caused by an STD. A test revealed that Nakeesha had chlamydia, a sexually transmitted disease common among teens.

Now Nakeesha wonders what effect her STD will have on her unborn baby's health and well-being. She doesn't think she can talk to Sergio about this problem, but the doctor says that he, too, must get treatment, or Nakeesha will probably get sick again.

CELESTE, SIXTEEN YEARS OLD

Sixteen-year-old Celeste is president of her sophomore class in high school. At the end of Celeste's freshman year, she went to a party at a friend's house where somebody brought alcohol along with the chips and videos. Somehow things got out of hand, and Celeste ended up having sex in a bedroom upstairs with a guy she barely knew.

Later that summer, while getting a sports physical, Celeste asked her doctor about some embarrassing symptoms she was having. After a test or two, he told her that she had gonorrhea, a sexually transmitted disease. Celeste was shocked. She had heard of gonorrhea, but she had always believed that only prostitutes and promiscuous girls could catch it. Now she had to revise her opinions. She realized that she didn't know very much about sexually transmitted diseases after all.

LEAH AND DANIEL, SEVENTEEN YEARS OLD

Leah and Daniel met each other at the end of their sophomore year. They have dated for three months and talk about getting married as soon as they graduate. For Daniel, however, two years seems like a long time to wait to have sex. Leah is willing to be patient, but wants to please Daniel more than anything else.

Leah decided to share her mixed feelings with her older sister, Susan. Susan suggested that Leah visit a doctor or health clinic to get information on birth control before going "all the way." At the clinic, a nurse/counselor gave Leah literature and condoms (close-fitting rubber coverings worn over the penis during sexual intercourse to prevent pregnancy or the spread of STDs), and suggested that both she and Daniel be tested for STDs before taking the next step.

Leah thinks it's a good suggestion, but Daniel thinks she's making a big to-do about nothing.

NATHAN, NINETEEN YEARS OLD

Nathan has lived on the streets of Seattle since he ran away from home two years ago. Like many of his street friends, he turned to prostitution to live and to support his drug use.

One night last year, Nathan was beaten up by one of his customers and ended up in the hospital. There, a doctor broke the news that Nathan tested positive for *human immunodeficiency virus* (HIV), the virus that causes AIDS. Nathan was shocked, but he pretended the news didn't bother him. He accepted the medications the doctor gave him, even took them regularly for a while. Only after two of Nathan's friends died of drug overdoses in the same week, however, did he begin to reevaluate his behavior and the direction and purpose of his life.

MIGUEL AND LARISSA, EIGHTEEN YEARS OLD

Larissa is Miguel's dream girl—tall, beautiful, and intelligent. More importantly, she seems to love Miguel very much. Miguel has been intimate with his last two girlfriends, and he's hoping that Larissa will want to have sex with him soon. He's a little nervous, however. Some alarming growths on his penis have recently been diagnosed as genital warts, an STD caused by a virus. The doctor he went to told him that the warts were incurable and highly infectious, and Miguel should always wear a condom during sex. Even then, there would be no guarantee that he would not infect his partner.

Miguel knows he would feel bad if he gave Larissa genital warts. Still, he doesn't know if he'll do anything about the situation. "I guess I'm not sure it's that big a deal," he says. But he looks embarrassed and thoughtful.

Knowledge can make a real difference in how young people behave when it comes to issues such as sex, pregnancy, drug abuse, and the like. Understanding STDs—their prevalence, their symptoms, how they're passed and how they can be treated—is an important first step in bringing under control a problem that affects millions of teens like Nakeesha, Celeste, Daniel, and Miguel every year in the United States.

In the following chapters, you will have the opportunity to learn about the principal STDs that affect young people today. The book will make clear how to avoid catching these diseases, and how to have a meaningful life even if you catch one for which there is no cure. First, however, it is important to be familiar with the kind of behavior and attitudes that put teens at risk for catching STDs. "It's not kiddie land out there," Nathan observes. "You have to be careful with sex or you can pay a high price. Just ask me. But you don't have to be as stupid as I was."

Chapter One

WHY WORRY?

- Do you know that you could have an STD and not know it?
- Do you know that, in the United States, teens are at the highest risk for getting an STD?
- Do you know that you can catch an STD without "going all the way"?
- Do you know that women are more at risk than men for catching some STDs?

Sexually transmitted diseases were once known as venereal diseases, named after Venus, the Roman goddess of love. They have infected humankind for centuries. The Greek physician Galen gave gonorrhea its name in the second century A.D., and the disease was well known to the ancient Chinese and Egyptians. Syphilis was the scourge of Europe from the sixteenth through the nineteenth centuries, killing hundreds of thousands of people in terrifying *epidemics*. Although recognized as physical afflictions, neither gonorrhea nor syphilis was well understood, however. For a time, they were even believed to be one disease, probably because people were often infected with both at the same time.

The discovery of antibiotics in the 1930s and 1940s provided a cure for people suffering from gonorrhea and syphilis, and doctors believed that the diseases would soon be wiped out. In fact, such was not the case. Both infections have continued to trouble humans over time, sustained by poverty, poor public education, and a host of social factors.

A FRIGHTENING PROBLEM

Our ancestors recognized only two major STDs—syphilis and gonorrhea—but today there are more than twenty known diseases that can be transmitted sexually. Some, such as chancroid and Donovanosis, are rare in the United States. Others such as trichomoniasis, an infection that causes discharge, burning, and itching, are common, but more irritating than dangerous. Fortunately, fewer than half of the known STDs pose serious threats to public health in the United States. Still, sexually transmitted diseases infect humans in record numbers today. The United States leads the world in the rate of STDs contracted, with more than 12 million new cases reported annually in the late 1990s.

Why should teens worry about those figures? The answer is simple and frightening. About one quarter of those 12 million cases—roughly 3 million—involve teenagers, who have the highest rate of STD infection for any age group in the United States. More than 6 million cases involve people under the age of twenty-five. Young people are becoming sexually active at younger and younger ages, and STD infections are threatening their ability to have children, increasing their risk of cancer and other diseases, even threatening their lives.

WHY HAVEN'T STDs DISAPPEARED?

In the age of antibiotics and modern medicine, why do STDs continue to pose a threat to human health? There are a variety of reasons, which include:

Lack of Information

Educating people about STDs has always been difficult. Many Americans believe that anything relating to sex is a private topic, and talking about it is in bad taste. Some have never been taught about sex and don't want to reveal their ignorance. Some adults don't talk to their children about sexual matters because they believe that young people who are informed are more likely to be sexually active.

Sex education classes in schools usually offer comprehensive information about STDs, but these classes are sometimes boring or preachy. Students are often turned off by the way material is presented and tune it out. Some teens do not attend class regularly or drop out of school and miss the message altogether. Televised public-service announcements about the risks of STDs are more attention getting, but they can only give general advice rather than detailed, accurate information about preventing STDs or getting treatment if you have one.

Embarrassment

Many people don't talk about STDs with partners because they are embarrassed. It is hard to bring up a discussion of sex with someone you're trying to impress, someone you're not sure likes you, or someone you're afraid you might offend. STDs are even more difficult to talk about because they carry the suggestion of promiscuity and disease. Thus, too many teens have sex first and then find out the sexual history of their partner when it may be too late.

Poverty

People who are poor are often uneducated and have never learned the facts about STDs. Even if they suspect they have an infection, they are not used to going to doctors, or cannot afford them, and so do not seek treatment. Some poor people are suspicious of authorities, and so they stay away from health clinics that provide information and treatment, even if those clinics are free.

Ethnic and Religious Taboos

Religious beliefs and traditions that condemn premarital sex, promiscuity, adultery, and other sexual behavior as "sin" discourage discussions of the problem of STDs. Religious advocates tend to adhere to the belief that if teens just avoid sexual behavior, they do not need to know the facts about STDs and safer sex.

Some religious groups discourage the use of condoms because they believe that the use of birth-control devices is wrong. In some ethnic groups, women do not have the right to question their partner's sexual activities or even the right to demand that safer sex be practiced.

All such customs make the control of STDs more difficult and increase the risk that these infections will be passed from person to person.

Media Messages

At the same time that many people hesitate to talk about sex, music, movies, and television fill the airways with messages that sex is irresistible, trouble free, and fun. Characters in a multitude of sitcoms think about sex, joke about sex, and have casual sexual encounters all the time without worrying much about the physical consequences of their actions. In their storybook lives,

FACT OR FICTION?

With too little communication and too much misinformation about sex and sexually transmitted diseases in our world today, how much do you know about STDs? The following is a list of several commonly held beliefs. Decide which are true and which are false.

1. I can tell by looking if someone is likely to have an STD.

   False. STDs do not discriminate against anyone. Even the cleanest, most well kept, and attractive person could be infected.

2. I'm not likely to get an STD the first time I have sex.

   True and False. On one hand, the majority of teens don't have STDs, so the odds are in your favor that you will have sex with someone who is not infected. On the other hand, there is no guarantee and no way to tell if you'll be safe. Many teens have contracted an STD during their first sexual encounter.

3. My new boyfriend/girlfriend hasn't been sexually active long enough to be infected with an STD.

   False. Only one prior sexual experience is needed to become infected. Teens are not too young to have STDs.

4. If my partner and I really love each other and have waited to have sex for several months, we don't have to worry about STDs.

   False. Being in a loving relationship doesn't mean that one or the other of you hasn't been infected in a previous sexual encounter.

5. If I'm healthy, I can't catch STDs.

   False. Although a strong immune system seems to help protect you from disease, even healthy people can catch STDs.

6. Being on the Pill protects me from STDs.

   False. Birth-control pills are an effective means of preventing pregnancy, but they do not provide the physical barrier necessary to protect the reproductive tract from bacteria and viruses that cause STDs.

7. My church doesn't believe in using birth-control devices such as condoms; sincere faith will protect me from catching an STD.

   False. Religious convictions have not been proven to be adequate protection against STDs.

8. If I wash thoroughly with soap and hot water immediately after sex, I won't catch an STD.

   False. Washing thoroughly with soap and hot water only slightly reduces the risk of catching an STD.

9. I'll know if I have an STD.

   False. Many STDs have no symptoms, particularly in women.

10. If I get an STD, I'll just take some penicillin and get rid of it.

    True and False. The treatment depends on the type of STD you have. Some STDs respond well to antibiotics, others are incurable.

they deal with broken hearts and unrequited love, but they seldom if ever cope with the complications of an STD such as herpes or genital warts. The message that comes across is that everyone is having sexual encounters, but nobody is worrying about the complications and responsibilities that go along with such encounters. Why should you?

More Numerous Sexual Contacts

As a result of a dramatic shift in social values in recent decades, more people are having more sexual contacts than ever before. This applies to teens as well. Most sexually active teens describe themselves as *monogamous*—that is, faithful to the person that they are in love with—but their feelings and their relationships are apt to change fairly rapidly, and they can have several partners in the course of a relatively short period of time.

More sexual contact means there are more opportunities to transfer disease from one person to another, especially since many people do not take precautions to minimize the spread of STDs when they have casual sex. Many teens feel that sex should be a romantic and passionate experience, and they feel guilty if they deliberately plan for it. "I'd feel like a slut if I carried a condom around all the time," says one seventeen-year-old girl. "Like all I'm thinking about is sex."

Misplaced Trust

Teens often believe that trusting a boyfriend or girlfriend is more important than behaving carefully when it comes to sex. "Most people don't know much about STDs unless they've had one—and even if they've had one, they sometimes don't know a lot," states one teen. "A lot of people feel that if you don't have symptoms, then you don't have to worry about it, and a lot of people trust their partners."

Trust can be misplaced, however. In at least one study, young men admit that they lied about their sexual past—downplayed the number of partners they have had or whether they have had an STD—in order to get a girl to have sex with them. Some even said that they would lie about having been tested for AIDS in order to have sex.

Alcohol and Drugs

Alcohol and drug use often leads to risky behavior that can put teens at high risk for STDs. One study of more than 34,000 teens found that those who drank were seven times more likely to have sex than their peers who abstained, and teens under fifteen who used drugs were almost four times more likely to have sex than those who did not use drugs. "If you believe in abstinence [refraining from having sex], you should know that it can be undermined by alcohol and drug use," states one of the authors of the study.

Under the influence of alcohol and drugs, sexual encounters are often casual, unplanned, and unprotected. Since drinkers may have impaired judgment, they are less likely to worry about STDs or safer sex.

Denial

Despite the AIDS epidemic, many teens still do not believe that they will catch HIV or any other STD. They think they are not old enough or promiscuous enough to become infected. They think that STDs strike only certain groups such as homosexuals, prostitutes, the poor, or people in other countries.

Some teens mistakenly assume that nothing bad can ever happen to them. "We're dealing with the basic psychology of adolescents, who believe 'it isn't going to happen to me,'" says one health care expert. "It's why they smoke, why they don't wear seat belts, and why they're at risk for STDs."

I'm Infected Where?

A final reason that STDs continue to trouble both adults and teens is that they affect a portion of the human body—the reproductive organs, or *genitals*—that is considered very personal and private. Many people do not touch or examine their genitals, and thus fail to discover a telltale blister or sore. If they notice a symptom, they may ignore it and hope it will go away rather than face an embarrassing interlude with a doctor.

It is always easier to discuss a problem if one knows the right words to use. The following section will help readers gain some familiarity with terms that describe parts of the male and female reproductive systems. Such knowledge will also aid in later discussions of symptoms and complications.

THE MALE REPRODUCTIVE SYSTEM

Most male reproductive organs are located outside the body. A primary organ, the *penis*, is a tube-shaped structure through which runs a smaller tube called the *urethra*. The urethra serves a dual purpose: It carries urine from the bladder and *sperm* (male sex cells) from the *testicles*. When a male is sexually excited or aroused, the penis becomes large and stiff so that it can be easily inserted into a female's vagina.

Two other primary reproductive organs, the testicles, lie behind and below the penis. They are egg-shaped and encased in a loose sac of skin called the *scrotum*. The testicles produce testosterone, a male hormone, as well as sperm. Small tubules known as the *epididymis* and the *vas deferens* carry sperm from the testicles to the urethra. During ejaculation, sperm are transported out of the penis in *semen*, a fluid produced by the *prostate gland* and the *seminal vesicles*, both of

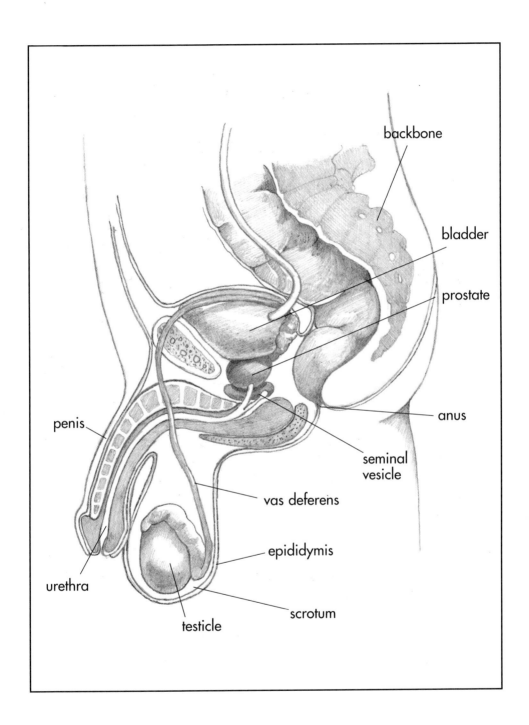

backbone

bladder

prostate

penis

anus

seminal
vesicle

vas deferens

epididymis

urethra

scrotum

testicle

23

which are located inside the body, near the bladder and in front of the large intestine.

The intestinal opening, which lies behind the testicles and scrotum and between the buttocks, is termed the *anus*. It is not technically part of the reproductive system, but can sometimes be affected by sexually transmitted diseases.

THE FEMALE REPRODUCTIVE SYSTEM

Many of the female reproductive organs are located inside the body. The *uterus* is a muscular, pear-shaped organ that lies in the lower abdomen between the bladder and the large intestine. During pregnancy, the uterus stretches to allow for the growth of the baby inside. The lower end of the uterus is called the *cervix*. Set to either side of the uterus are the *ovaries*, where eggs (female sex cells) and estrogen, a female hormone, are produced. Encircling the ovaries are the *fallopian tubes*, through which a mature egg travels on its way to the uterus. The uterus opens into the *vagina*, through which a baby passes to the outside during birth. An external reproductive structure in the female is the *vulva*, which consists of the inner and outer *labia*, fleshy folds of skin, and the *clitoris*, the organ of sexual arousal about the size of a raisin that sits in front of the vaginal opening.

The urethra, through which urine passes from the bladder, is not part of the reproductive system in the female. The urethra passes in front of the vagina and ends in a tiny opening between the clitoris and the vagina. The anus, the opening of the large intestine, lies behind the vulva and between the buttocks. As in the male, both the urethra and the anus can be affected by STDs.

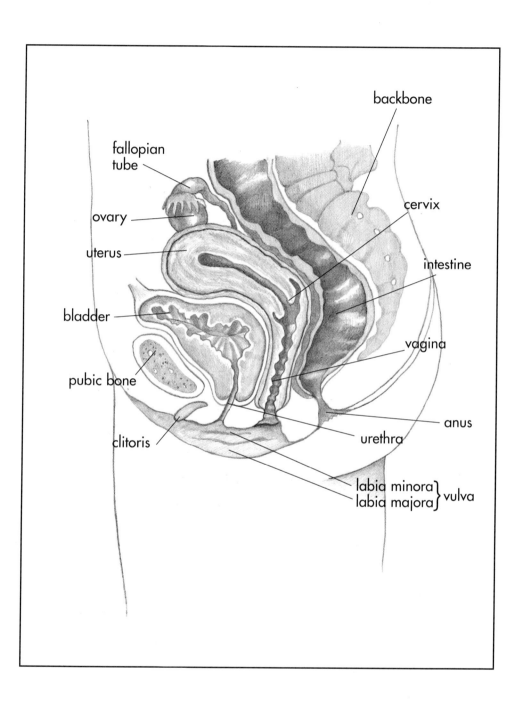

fallopian
tube

ovary

uterus

bladder

pubic bone

clitoris

backbone

cervix

intestine

vagina

anus

urethra

labia minora
labia majora } vulva

RATE YOUR RISK

Now that you understand why STDs still trouble people in modern times, you can decide for yourself if you are at risk for catching an STD. Answer the following questions, tally your score, and see if you are taking unnecessary chances with your health and future.

1. Have you or your partner ever shared needles while using *intravenous* drugs (drugs injected in a vein)?

    yes (15 pts)   no (0 pts)

Sharing needles or having sex with someone who uses intravenous drugs greatly increases your risk of contracting AIDS and hepatitis B.

2. Have you ever had sexual intercourse?

    yes (2 pts)   no (0 pts)

If you abstain from having sexual intercourse, you are at low risk of catching an STD.

Do not answer the following if you answered NO to question #2.

3. Do you ever have sex without using a condom?

    yes (2 pts)   no (1 pt)

Not using a condom every time you have sex puts you at high risk for catching an STD.

4. Do you have sex during or after using drugs or alcohol?

    yes (2 pts)   no (1 pt)

Having sex while drinking or using drugs lowers your inhibitions and can lead to sexual risk taking.

5. Do you have sex with people you don't know well?
      yes (2 pts)   no (1 pt)

   It can be very dangerous to have sex with someone whose sexual past is unknown to you.

6. Have you had sex with more than one partner in the last three months?
      yes (2 pts)   no (1 pt)

   Every time you have sex with a new partner, you raise the odds that you could catch an STD.

7. Do you know or think that your partner has had sex with other partners?
      yes (2 pts)   no (1 pt)

   When you have sex with someone, it's like having sex with all their former partners, too.

8. Have you ever had sex with someone in exchange for money or drugs?
      yes (2 pts)   no (1 pt)

   Having sex for drugs or money is very risky behavior.

9. Are you. . .
      male (1 pt)
      female (2 pts)?

   Due to anatomical differences, females are at greater risk of catching STDs than men.

10. Are you . . .
      under 25 years old (2 pts)
      25 or older (1 pt)?

   People under the age of twenty-five are at greater risk for catching STDs than people who are older.

If your total is below 10, your behavior puts you at little or no risk of catching an STD. If your score is 10–14, you have some risk of catching an STD. If you score above 14, some aspects of your behavior are putting you at high risk for catching an STD.

No matter what your risk, STDs remain a serious problem in the United States as the twenty-first century begins. It is wise to be well informed, to be knowledgeable about STDs that are likely to cause serious problems, to recognize their symptoms (if any), and to understand what to do if you suspect you're infected.

This book presents information on the seven most common and health-threatening STDs in the United States—chlamydia, gonorrhea, syphilis, herpes, acquired immune deficiency syndrome (AIDS), genital warts, and hepatitis B. A discussion of one of the most common, chlamydia, begins in the next chapter.

Chapter Two

WHAT YOU SHOULD KNOW ABOUT CHLAMYDIA

NAKEESHA AND SERGIO

Nakeesha and Sergio are both seventeen. Both dropped out of high school last year. Sergio works full-time and Nakeesha stays home to take care of their one-year-old daughter, Alicia. Nakeesha was planning to go to an alternative school this year to get her general equivalency diploma (GED), but she is pregnant again and feels nauseous every morning.

A short time ago, Nakeesha also began to suffer from pain in her lower abdomen. She had chills and thought she might have a fever. "At first I thought the pain was gas, you know, and then I thought maybe it was the baby. Sergio thought maybe I just had the flu. He didn't think it was nothing serious," she says. Because she and Sergio have little money to pay for doctor's visits, she put up with the problem until her regular monthly checkup a week later.

The doctor thought the tenderness in Nakeesha's abdomen might be an inflamed appendix or an ovarian cyst. Because she was sexually active and pregnant, however, he tested her for STDs. The test revealed that she had pelvic inflammatory disease, a potentially serious infection of the upper reproductive tract. The infection stemmed from Nakeesha's primary problem— chlamydia, a common STD among young, sexually active women. "I never heard of it before," Nakeesha admits. "Maybe they taught about it in health class, but I guess I didn't pay much attention."

Because she was pregnant, Nakeesha was hospitalized and treated with antibiotics. When Sergio came to visit her, she told him that he, too, needed to be tested for chlamydia. "He didn't want to," Nakeesha says. "He said he didn't have no symptoms. He felt fine. But the doctor insisted." To Sergio's surprise, his test was positive for chlamydia, too.

A teenage girl infected with chlamydia has a one in eight chance of developing pelvic inflammatory disease (PID). After the age of twenty-four, her risk drops to one in eighty.

Now recovered, Nakeesha thinks back on her infection. Having been with no one but Sergio, she knows that she got chlamydia from him, and wonders how he caught a sexually transmitted disease. She would like to talk to him about it, but doesn't think she can. "He says lots of his friends have had clap (gonorrhea) before, and this kind of stuff is no big thing. I want to believe him," she says. Still, she worries that Sergio is not being faithful, and that she may become infected with something more serious next time.

WHAT IS CHLAMYDIA?

Chlamydia (pronounced cluh-MID-ee-ah) was first recognized as an STD by medical experts about 1970. At the close of the twentieth century, it was the most common, fastest-spreading, nonviral STD in the United States. Caused by a tiny bacteria, *Chlamydia trachomatis* (*C. trachomatis*), it can infect the urinary-genital area, the anal area, and sometimes the eyes, throat, and lungs.

In 1998 more than 600,000 new cases of chlamydia were reported to the Centers for Disease Control and Prevention (CDC), America's top public-health agency. Because a large number of people do not know they have chlamydia, however, the agency estimates that the number of those infected annually is closer to 4 million. Various studies show that up to 50 percent of symptom-free individuals who are randomly tested for chlamydia test positive for the bacteria.

Anyone who has more than one sexual partner, has a new sexual partner, fails to use condoms regularly, and/or has a gonorrhea infection is at high risk for chlamydia, but the highest rates of infection are among female teens. This seems to be because the tissue of their cervix is thinner, making them more vulnerable to infection. Experts estimate that one out of every ten teenage girls may be infected with chlamydia.

HOW IS CHLAMYDIA TRANSMITTED?

Chlamydia is easy to transmit through oral, genital, or anal sex with an infected partner. The bacteria is carried in semen and vaginal fluids. Chlamydia primarily infects the mucous membranes of the cervix in women and the urethra in men, although it can also infect other mucous membranes as well.

Chlamydia can be passed from mother to baby as the baby passes through the vagina. About 50 percent of babies born to infected mothers acquire chlamydial eye infections, and about 10 percent develop lung infections. Such infections can lead to blindness, permanent lung damage, or death from pneumonia.

Kissing is not a risk factor in transmitting chlamydia, and infection is not passed on towels, toilet seats, bedding, or other inanimate objects.

WHAT ARE THE SYMPTOMS OF CHLAMYDIA?

People often experience no symptoms when they are infected with chlamydia. One half of infected men and three quarters of infected women are completely symptom free and are usually surprised when they are told they have tested positive. A person can be symptom free for life, or symptoms can develop weeks, months, or years after infection takes place.

For those individuals who do have symptoms, these are usually mild. Women may experience a frequent need to urinate, burning during urination, genital irritation, and yellowish-green vaginal discharge. In males, symptoms include a clear, thin discharge from the penis, burning with urination, an itchy or irritated

> A teen who is sexually active and not involved in a long-term, monogamous relationship should be tested periodically for chlamydia.

feeling in the urethra, and redness at the tip of the penis. In both sexes, symptoms usually disappear about three weeks after exposure.

Chlamydial eye infections produce conjunctivitis—redness, itching, and pain. With infections of the anal area, symptoms may include pain, discharge, and bleeding. Chlamydia of the throat, contracted during oral sex, may produce no symptoms, or may appear as a sore throat.

ARE THERE COMPLICATIONS FROM CHLAMYDIA?

Serious complications can arise when a chlamydia infection goes untreated. In men this can include infection of the prostate gland and epididymis resulting in scarring and *infertility* (the inability to have children). In women, infection can and often does spread to the uterus, fallopian tubes, and ovaries, a serious condition known as pelvic inflammatory disease (PID). Scarring from PID can lead to infertility or *ectopic pregnancies.*

> Many people discover they have had a chlamydia infection when they are unable to have children, and then it is too late. Be tested early and regularly to help safeguard your health and fertility!

Ectopic pregnancy, in which a fertilized egg implants in the fallopian tubes instead of the lining of the uterus, can lead to pain, significant bleeding, and even death.

A person can become infected with chlamydia repeatedly, and recurrent chlamydial infections usually are more severe, with greater likelihood of pelvic inflammatory disease. With each episode of PID, a woman has a 20 percent reduction in her chances of having children, as well as a 20 percent increased chance of chronic pelvic pain and ectopic pregnancy.

Reiter's syndrome, a condition involving recurrent episodes of urethritis (infection of the urethra), arthritis, conjunctivitis, skin rashes, and other symptoms, is a rare complication that occurs in some people with chlamydia. This syndrome may reoccur even after the infection has been treated with antibiotics, and seems to be the body's mistaken attempt to fight off infection by attacking normal tissues. Experts are unclear why some people develop Reiter's syndrome. They believe there may be a genetic predisposition for the condition.

HOW DOES A DOCTOR DIAGNOSE CHLAMYDIA?

Testing for chlamydia is not a routine part of a regular physical checkup, and a doctor may not think to suggest that a teen have a diagnostic test. Often the first time a woman is diagnosed as having had chlamydia is when she cannot become pregnant later in life, after scarring of the fallopian tubes has taken place.

Once a person decides to be tested, there are several procedures from which to choose. A health-care provider can help decide which is the best for each individual. The culture method involves a doctor taking a swab of material from the cervix or a small swab of fluid from the penis. The sample is cultured (allowed to grow) in special nutrient solution in a lab, and bacteria are looked for under a microscope. Culture tests are also used to diagnose throat and anal infections.

A doctor may also take a blood or urine sample and order non-culture tests such as the *enzyme-linked immunosorbent assay* (ELISA) and tests that involve the *polymerase chain reaction* (PCR), which look directly for bacterial genetic material. These tests are more accurate, but they are also more expensive.

WHAT IS THE TREATMENT FOR CHLAMYDIA?

Once diagnosed, chlamydia can be cured with antibiotic treatment. For an uncomplicated infection, doctors will commonly prescribe an antibiotic such as azithromycin, doxycycline, or erythromycin. With PID or infection of the epididymis or prostate, a longer course of medication is usually necessary. Although antibiotics can kill all chlamydia bacteria, they cannot reverse the aftereffects of PID such as scarring and chronic pain.

Erythromycin is usually prescribed for pregnant women who are infected with chlamydia, since other antibiotics may be harmful to the unborn child. With treatment, there is almost no risk that a baby will be born with chlamydia. "My first thought was for my baby," Nakeesha says. "I was really worried that I'd hurt it in some way. I guess it could have been seriously hurt if I hadn't gotten treatment, but the doctor says it should be all right now." To help ensure that newborns do not develop chlamydial eye infections, hospitals routinely treat all babies' eyes with antibiotic ointment shortly after birth.

Until a physician determines that an individual is infection free, all sexual contact should be avoided. It is important that all of an infected person's partners be checked and treated for chlamydia, whether or not they have symptoms. (In many states, it is mandatory to

> In many states a teen does not need parental consent to be tested and treated for an STD.

report chlamydia infections to the state health department.) Follow-up testing is important, to ensure that the infection has disappeared completely. "The key message for chlamydia is that it is a fully preventable and fully curable disease," says an expert at the CDC.

The same can be said of gonorrhea and syphilis, two more bacterial STDs that continue to infect American teenagers. These two infections will be discussed in depth in Chapter Three.

WHAT YOU SHOULD KNOW ABOUT GONORRHEA AND SYPHILIS

CELESTE

No one would ever pick Celeste as a candidate for an STD infection. Not only is she president of her sophomore class, she is always busy with volunteer work and running track, and manages to be one of the top students in her high school. Freckle-faced and a little awkward, she has lots of friends, but no boyfriends. On weekends, she concentrates on her studies and watching old movies on TV.

Last June a friend invited Celeste to a party to celebrate the end of the school year. At the party some of the boys sneaked in some beer, and when Kurtis, one of the cutest boys on the track team, offered Celeste a bottle, she couldn't resist. After that, it seemed easier for Celeste to talk to Kurtis. They flirted and laughed, and one thing led to another. Celeste knew that other girls sometimes had sex at parties, but she never thought that she'd be one of them.

The incident wasn't as romantic as she'd thought it would be, and she was embarrassed afterward that she'd become intimate with Kurtis. "It was the first time I had ever been physical with anyone," she says. "At the time Kurtis seemed irresistible, but afterward I just felt stupid. I promised myself I would wait until I was really in love before it happened again. Then I tried to forget about it."

Celeste was not going to easily forget her first sexual encounter, however. When she went to her family doctor for a sports physical in late July, she mentioned to him that she was having pain and itching when she urinated. She was also spotting between her periods. The doctor did a pelvic exam and took a swab from her cervix. The sample showed that Celeste was infected with gonorrhea.

"The room started spinning!" she says. "The doctor was really professional and nonjudgmental and gave me a prescription, but I had to tell who I'd had sexual contact with. Cases of gonorrhea have to be reported to the state health department. And I tried, but I couldn't hide the prescription from my parents. They were mad at Kurtis and disappointed in me. It was a real mess."

WHAT IS GONORRHEA?

Gonorrhea, sometimes called "clap," is another very common STD in the United States. It is caused by the bacterium *Neisseria gonorrhoeae* (*N. gonorrhoeae*), which produces a number of genital infections and can also infect the mouth, throat, and anal area.

More than 350,000 cases of gonorrhea were reported to the CDC in 1998. Some experts estimate that the number of actual cases may be more than twice as high, however. Infection rates are dropping for adults, but rising for teens and people under the age of twenty-four. Sexually active teens living in high-density urban areas are at greatest risk, but anyone who has multiple partners, and/or engages in unprotected sex, can catch gonorrhea.

HOW IS GONORRHEA TRANSMITTED?

Gonorrhea is very easy to catch and is transmitted through sexual contact with an infected partner and through oral sex. The bacteria are carried in infected discharge, semen, and vaginal fluids. Gonorrhea commonly infects the mucous membranes of the urethra in males and the cervix in females, although other mucous membranes can be infected as well. Women are more at risk than males, perhaps because infected semen remains in the vagina after intercourse, creating a wider

> A person infected with an STD should stop having sexual relations until a doctor determines that all signs of infection are gone. Otherwise a partner can be infected.

window of opportunity for infection. A male who has unprotected sex with an infected female has a 20–30 percent chance of catching gonorrhea, but a woman who has unprotected sex with an infected male has a 60–80 percent chance of becoming infected. Gonorrhea can be passed from an infected woman to her infant during delivery, but it cannot be passed on inanimate objects such as toilet seats and towels.

WHAT ARE THE SYMPTOMS OF GONORRHEA?

About 10 percent of men and more than 50 percent of women have no symptoms when they catch gonorrhea.

For those who do experience symptoms, these usually develop within two to ten days of sexual contact with an infected partner. A few people may experience symptoms as early as one day after infection, while some may feel nothing for several weeks. "I started having symptoms pretty soon after the party, but they were mild," Celeste remembers. "I hoped they would go away. It was so embarrassing talking about them to the doctor."

Celeste experienced typical symptoms of gonorrhea. In a female, these include pain or burning during urination, yellow or bloody vaginal discharge, and/or spotting between menstrual periods and after intercourse. In males, the most common symptom is discharge from the penis and a moderate to severe burning sensation during urination. Discharge is usually yellow and heavy, although it can be clear and almost unnoticeable.

Both men and women can experience gonorrheal infection in the anal area, marked by pain, itching, discharge, and bleeding. Gonorrhea of the throat, contracted during oral sex, may produce no symptoms, or may appear as a sore throat. Redness and a thick yellow discharge mark a gonorrheal eye infection, most common in newborns.

ARE THERE COMPLICATIONS FROM GONORRHEA?

Complications that can develop from gonorrhea are usually painful and more serious than the initial infection. As is the case with chlamydia, infection in women can develop into pelvic inflammatory disease (PID)

Gonorrhea infections can lead to infertility, the inability to have children.

with all its attendant risks (see Chapter Two). Gonorrhea can also infect the abdominal area and cause pain and inflammation around the liver, a condition known as Fitz-Hugh-Curtis syndrome. Women who become infected with gonorrhea while they are pregnant run a risk of miscarriage and premature delivery.

In men, complications of gonorrhea can include infection of the prostate, which causes pain between the testicles and the anal area. If the epididymis becomes infected, scarring can impair a man's ability to have children and can even cause infertility.

Very rarely, gonorrhea can spread through the bloodstream to other parts of the body, causing disseminated gonococcal infection (DGI). Symptoms include fever, chills, joint pain, rashes, endocarditis (infection of the heart valves), and meningitis (infection of the lining of the brain and spinal cord).

HOW DOES A DOCTOR DIAGNOSE GONORRHEA?

Testing for gonorrhea must always involve a doctor's examination. For males, the doctor will commonly use the Gram's stain test, during which a sample of discharge is taken from the urethra, placed on a slide, and stained with dye. The slide is then examined for bacteria under a microscope. For females, culture tests may give more accurate results. In these, a sample of discharge from the urethra or the cervix is brushed across a nutrient medium, allowed to grow for forty-eight hours, then examined under the microscope. The success of the test relies on there being enough bacteria on the swab to culture.

Because microscopic examinations sometimes miss infections, more sensitive procedures that detect the genes of the bacteria are becoming widely used. They are usually more accurate, but they can be more expensive.

WHAT IS THE TREATMENT FOR GONORRHEA?

Gonorrhea can readily be cured with antibiotics. For years penicillin was the drug of choice, but cases of resistant bacteria (that is, bacteria that are not killed by penicillin and other antibiotics) have become more common over time. Patients are often given a single dose injection of ceftriaxone or a single dose of such oral medications as ofloxacin, cefixime, or ciprofloxacin.

> Be sure to take STD medication for the length of time prescribed, even if symptoms disappear. Otherwise an STD infection can return in a more serious form.

For more complicated infections such as PID or endocarditis, a longer course of treatment and hospitalization may be necessary.

Gonorrhea must be reported to the health department in most states to ensure that all sexual partners are contacted and receive treatment. A follow-up examination is important to ensure that treatment has been fully effective.

WHAT IS SYPHILIS?

Syphilis, another STD from the past, is caused by the bacterium *Treponema pallidum* (*T. pallidum*). Because of its spiral shape, the bacterium is called a spirochete. Known as the "great imitator," syphilis can mimic a variety of diseases and can affect virtually every part of the body.

Less prevalent than gonorrhea, only about seven thousand new cases of syphilis were reported to the CDC in the United States in 1998. Teens should not dismiss the disease as irrelevant to their lives, however. Rates of syphilis remain high in regions of the United States where poverty, lack of education, and inadequate access to health care contribute to higher rates of infection.

HOW IS SYPHILIS TRANSMITTED?

Like gonorrhea, syphilis is transmitted through sexual contact—vaginal, oral, or anal—with an infected partner. Sources of infection are syphilitic sores, rashes, and *lesions*, and possibly blood, semen, and vaginal secretions. Bacteria enter an uninfected person's body by passing through mucous membranes or through tiny breaks in the skin. The microbes are easily transmitted.

> People can transmit syphilis even when they have no symptoms.

On average, a person has a one in three chance of contracting syphilis from a single unprotected sexual contact with an infected person.

Syphilis often crosses the placental barrier and infects an unborn *fetus*. Results of such infection can be very serious. Almost half of untreated infected women will have a stillbirth (a baby dead at birth) or will deliver a baby that dies shortly after birth. Babies who live have up to a 70 percent chance of having congenital syphilis (syphilis existing at or before birth).

There is no evidence that syphilis is passed on toilet seats, swimming pools, hot tubs, bathtubs, shared clothing, or other inanimate objects.

WHAT ARE THE SYMPTOMS OF SYPHILIS?

Syphilic infection is divided into early and late stages, and symptoms vary depending on the stage.

The early stage of syphilis includes primary, secondary, and early latent periods. Primary syphilis starts at the moment of infection and lasts for several months. The first symptom is a single, painless sore termed a *chancre* (pronounced SHAN-ker). The chancre is small and round with raised edges, and appears between ten and ninety days (the average is three weeks) after infection. It arises at the point where the bacterium entered the body. This can be the penis or scrotum in males, the vagina in females, or the anus, lips, or tongue in either sex.

Many people miss the initial chancre because it is painless and is often in a nonvisible spot. Swollen lymph nodes in the genital area may signal that something is wrong, but these are painless as well, and so can go unnoticed. Symptoms usually disappear without treatment after a few weeks, and the infected person may never know he or she has syphilis.

Without treatment, secondary syphilis develops. During this period, bacteria enter the bloodstream and spread to other organs in the body. Persons are extremely infectious to partners at this stage and can even infect people through nonsexual contact with a break in the skin. Symptoms may be similar to the flu, and can also include:

- A rash characterized by brown sores, particularly on the palms of the hands and the soles of the feet
- Swollen lymph nodes
- Sore throat

- Joint pain
- Headache and fever
- Hair loss
- Wartlike lesions in the genital area

If the disease is not treated at this point, symptoms again disappear, and early latent syphilis begins. This period can last for decades, and can be detected only through blood tests. During this time, however, spirochetes multiply and spread into the circulatory system, central nervous system, brain, and bones. A person is commonly not infectious during this period.

Late stage or tertiary syphilis is rarely seen in modern times for two reasons. First, many people get treatment earlier in their infection. Second, 75 percent of people with long-term syphilis never show symptoms. If symptoms do occur, however, they are extremely serious. Tertiary syphilis can damage almost any organ or system in the body. *Neurosyphilis*, infection of the nervous system, can cause progressive paralysis. Other symptoms include mental illness (dementia), blindness, degeneration of the reflexes, vomiting, deep sores on the soles of the feet, and severe abdominal pain. Death can occur due to infection of the heart and major blood vessels.

Children who are born with syphilis (congenital syphilis) may have no symptoms, or a variety of problems that include failure to gain weight, fever, rashes, sores, bone lesions, and bone deformities. Complications such as deafness, blindness, bone pain, and deterioration of the central nervous system may appear later in life. Some typical, irreversible signs that a child has had congenital syphilis include a high forehead, no bridge to the nose (saddlenose) and peg-shaped teeth (Hutchinson's teeth).

HOW DOES A DOCTOR DIAGNOSE SYPHILIS?

There are several methods of diagnosing syphilis. A doctor may recognize physical symptoms such as a chancre, may microscopically identify bacteria swabbed from lesions, or may choose to draw a blood sample and order blood tests. The most common blood tests are the venereal disease research laboratory (VDRL) test and the rapid plasma reagin (RPR) test. Such tests will show a positive reaction within a few weeks of infection and will continue to do so unless a person receives treatment. Because these tests sometimes produce inaccurate results, the doctor may order a follow-up, commonly the fluorescent treponemal antibody-absorption (FTA-ABS) test. It is accurate in 70 to 90 percent of cases.

In many areas of the world, including parts of the United States, it is common for pregnant women to be tested for syphilis during a routine prenatal checkup. If a woman is treated during the first four months of her pregnancy, there is a very good chance that the unborn baby will not be infected with syphilis.

WHAT IS THE TREATMENT FOR SYPHILIS?

Most cases of syphilis, including congenital syphilis, can be cured with penicillin, although any damage done to body organs and systems cannot be reversed. In persons who have had an infection for less than a year, a single injection is usually sufficient. For long-term infections or for persons with neurosyphilis, a series of injections is necessary. Persons who are allergic to penicillin can be treated with other antibiotics. For pregnant women and infants, a specialist should oversee the course of treatment.

In all cases, follow-up blood tests to ensure that the bacteria are totally eliminated from the body are essential, especially if a person is also infected with HIV. Partners of an infected person must also be tested by a physician in order to determine their STD status and prevent further infection or reinfection.

New cases of syphilis must be reported to a state health department to ensure that all sexual partners are contacted and receive treatment. People do not develop *immunity* to gonorrhea and syphilis. Even if they have been infected before, they can become infected again and again, so periodic checkups are important in the case of high-risk behavior.

The next chapter deals with genital herpes, a viral STD that may at first seem preferable to gonorrhea and syphilis because it can be contracted only once. However, as author Jeffrey S. Nevid points out in his book *Choices*: "Once you get herpes, it's yours for life. . . . It remains an unwelcome guest in your body, finding a cozy place to lie low until it stirs up trouble again, causing recurrent outbreaks that usually happen at the worst times."

It doesn't pay to be ignorant about herpes. Read on to find out more about this troublesome and persistent STD.

Chapter Four

WHAT YOU SHOULD KNOW ABOUT GENITAL HERPES

LEAH AND DANIEL

Leah and Daniel are juniors in a small-town high school. They met in debate class during their sophomore year. Leah is flattered that Daniel likes her. He has been popular with the girls since seventh grade. There was even a rumor about his having a relationship with a college girl that he met at a drinking party last year.

Over the months, Leah and Daniel's physical relationship has escalated from kissing and holding hands to heavy petting, and Daniel has started pushing for more. "He's not doing any caveman stuff," Leah explains, "but he's pretty persistent. I come from a conservative family and sort of pictured myself waiting to go all the way until I was married. Dan doesn't understand. I'll probably do what he wants, but I'm afraid I'll get pregnant."

Leah has often shared her thoughts with her older sister Susan, and she has this time, too. Susan suggested that Leah get some information on birth control before she takes the next step. Both girls went to a health clinic in a nearby town, where a nurse informed Leah that birth-control pills would prevent pregnancy but not sexually transmitted diseases. She gave Leah some brochures and complimentary condoms. She also suggested that both Leah and Daniel be tested for STDs before they go any farther in their relationship.

Leah was embarrassed to talk to Daniel about condoms and STDs. She put it off for a few days. "I finally wrote him a note. I explained what the nurse had said, and asked him what he thought," she remembers.

The idea of using a condom bothered Daniel. "When I'm caught up in the moment, it just seems— you know—to kind of throw cold water on my feelings. It's a hassle," he explains. Leah agreed to compromise. She promised that she would go on birth-control pills— after all, neither of them wanted to start a family yet— and said she would forget about using condoms if Daniel would go in and be tested for STDs. Daniel reluctantly agreed.

Both Daniel and Leah were astounded when Daniel tested positive for herpes. "Yeah, I remember I had a few itchy blisters on my privates once about a year ago, but they didn't bother me much, and they never came back," he says. "Maybe I had herpes, but it's gone away now."

Leah is not convinced. She read the brochures and learned that herpes symptoms can come and go, but the infection remains. Daniel could still give her herpes. "I feel terrible," Leah says. "Dan's so mad at me for making him go through such an embarrassing experience. He says if I really love him, I won't let this come between us. But I don't know. I can't just forget that I could catch something that I'll have for the rest of my life."

WHAT IS GENITAL HERPES?

Before the advent of AIDS, genital herpes was the most feared STD in the modern world. Incurable and untreatable, it seemed to many to be a terrible punishment for the more casual sexual practices that had developed since the 1970s.

Today, most people understand that genital herpes is not a punishment for having sex. Nevertheless, the disease remains a painful and disruptive part of many people's lives. Caused by the herpes simplex type 2 virus (HSV-2), it is one of a family of viruses that cause cold sores, chicken pox, shingles, and mononucleosis. Herpes simplex type 1 virus (HSV-1), which causes oral herpes (cold sores), is a close relative of HSV-2. Oral herpes most commonly occurs around the face and is transmitted nonsexually through kissing or on the hands of someone who touches a cold sore. HSV-1 can sometimes infect the genital area, however. HSV-2 commonly infects the genitals, but can infect the face, throat, and eyes as well.

At the end of the twentieth century, there were an estimated 500,000 new cases of genital herpes in the United States each year. About 45 million people in the United States live with the virus (compared with about 100 million people who are infected with oral herpes), and because there is no cure, the numbers continue to rise. The chance of catching genital herpes during a single sexual encounter with a partner who is infectious is very high—about 50 percent for men and 80–90 percent for women.

Teens and young adults are at high risk because they tend to have more short-term sexual relationships with a number of partners. In the year 2000, genital herpes infections were five times more frequent among Caucasian teens than they were twenty years before.

HOW IS GENITAL HERPES TRANSMITTED?

Genital herpes can easily be transmitted through unprotected vaginal or anal intercourse or through oral sex. It can also be passed without intercourse if someone simply has genital-to-genital contact with a person who is infectious.

> One out of five people over the age of twelve is infected with genital herpes.

Herpes migrates from the skin down a nerve to a mass of nerve cells (ganglion) near the base of the spine. The virus can lay dormant in that ganglion for long periods of time. When it reactivates, it can travel through all the nerves that run out of the ganglion and surface on the skin and mucous membranes, producing blisters and lesions. These can occur on the genitals, buttocks, groin, and even the upper thighs.

Herpes can be transmitted from an infected mother to her baby as the baby passes through the birth canal during delivery. A woman who is infected before she becomes pregnant has antibodies in her bloodstream, which pass to the unborn baby and give it some protection from catching herpes at birth. The greatest risk to the unborn child comes if the mother catches herpes late in pregnancy. Then, there is up to a 50 percent chance that the baby will contract herpes at birth.

For the first few weeks of a herpes infection, before the body has time to build up immunity to the virus, infected persons can sometimes spread the virus to other parts of the body by touching the infected area and then immediately touching another part of the body. This phenomenon is called *autoinoculation* and is uncommon. In persons with weakened immune systems (such as those with AIDS) the virus can spread throughout the body, a process called *dissemination*. This, too, is rare.

The herpes virus is quickly inactivated when it dries, so there is little likelihood that it can be transmitted on dry towels, toilet seats, and other inanimate objects. Herpes cannot be caught in swimming pools or hot tubs unless someone has unprotected sex with an infected partner in one of those settings.

WHAT ARE THE SYMPTOMS OF GENITAL HERPES?

An estimated 20 percent of people who become infected with herpes never have symptoms and never know they are infected. Many of the remaining 80 percent, like Daniel, may not recognize their symptoms as herpes. All can pass their infection to others, however.

If symptoms develop, these usually first arise within two to twenty days of infection. Initial symptoms may be a bump or red area, and itching, burning, or tingling of the skin. These first symptoms are termed the *prodrome* period, and can serve as a warning to a herpes sufferer that he or she is very infectious and is going to have an outbreak (an occurrence of blisters).

> Herpes symptoms can occur on any area of the body supplied by an infected nerve.

Not every herpes sufferer experiences prodrome. Many go right into the *syndrome* period, when a variety of symptoms can occur. The most characteristic are blisters, usually about the size of a pinhead (but can be larger), which appear alone or in clusters. These can arise on the genitals, buttocks, groin, anal area, and pubic hair region. They are often itchy, but can also be very painful. Tiny slits or painful *ulcers* can form when

51

blisters burst. Blisters and sores that occur on skin surfaces usually scab over as they heal; those that occur on mucous membranes do not.

Other symptoms of herpes infection can include:

- Fever, nausea, chills, muscle aches, tiredness, and headaches
- Difficulty and/or pain during urination
- Swollen, painful lymph nodes in the groin
- Weakness, pain, or tenderness in the lower back, legs, groin, and buttocks
- Numbness in the genital area or lower back

Herpes symptoms normally last five to seven days, but may last as long as six weeks. They may be so slight that infected persons never realize they are having an outbreak. On the other hand, they can be very painful and traumatic, causing sufferers to miss work or school. "The doctor said that just because Daniel had mild symptoms, that was no guarantee that I would have mild symptoms if I caught herpes," Leah explains. "I could get really sick. It seems like it all depends on your chemical makeup and stuff like that."

Many infected individuals mistake their herpes symptoms for something else. For instance, they may experience pain during urination and believe they have a bladder infection or mistake vaginal discharge for a *yeast infection*. They may use antibiotics or over-the-counter yeast medications and think they have successfully treated their problem because the symptoms go away. In fact, the herpes infection has just subsided for a time and has the potential to recur later.

Women tend to experience more severe symptoms than men do. Persons with weakened immune systems generally have outbreaks that are longer and more severe as well. The primary episode of herpes is usually the most severe and takes longer to heal than later outbreaks.

> Herpes makes people more susceptible to HIV infection, and can make HIV-infected persons more infectious to their partners.

In some cases, herpes infections can become serious. The virus can inflame the lining of the spinal cord, causing viral meningitis. Symptoms include stiff neck and sensitivity to light. Oral herpes infections can cause encephalitis—inflammation of the brain—with headache, fever, and seizures. Half of babies who are infected with herpes at birth die or suffer permanent neurological damage. Others can develop serious problems that affect the brain, eyes, or skin.

WILL I ALWAYS HAVE SYMPTOMS OF HERPES?

Until experts find a cure or develop a vaccine, herpes remains an incurable infection. However, the first bout of symptoms normally disappears after about a week, and the virus can remain dormant for months at a time. Infected individuals feel perfectly healthy when they are symptom free, but they will have periods of asymptomatic *shedding* (shedding without symptoms) when the virus is present on their skin and can easily be passed to others. Everyone who has herpes will shed at some point between outbreaks. A person cannot know when asymptomatic shedding is occurring, but experts find that people seem to shed most frequently just before and after outbreaks. During outbreaks, a herpes sufferer experiences symptomatic shedding (shedding with symptoms) and is very infectious.

One of the unpleasant characteristics of genital herpes is that it is recurrent—that is, outbreaks can occur repeatedly. Some people cynically call it "the disease that keeps on giving." Symptoms appear at random times, often at the most untimely moments such as before a big test, at the beginning of a new relationship, or at the start of a new job. Some people experience eight or more outbreaks a year. The average is four or five. Over time, outbreaks usually become less frequent.

WHAT TRIGGERS HERPES OUTBREAKS?

Experts do not fully understand what causes the herpes virus to become active, but various factors seem to trigger outbreaks. These can include emotional and physical stress, fatigue, illness, certain kinds of food such as nuts or chocolate, hormonal changes related to menstruation and pregnancy, poor eating habits, trauma to the skin, or exposure to sunlight. Sometimes outbreaks occur even when sufferers do everything they can to avoid triggering the virus.

WHAT ABOUT THE EMOTIONAL
SIDE EFFECTS OF HERPES?

The emotional and psychological ramifications of genital herpes can be more distressing than its physical symptoms. Many people are deeply disturbed to learn that they have an incurable, contagious disease that can recur at any time. They feel anxious and guilty, knowing that they can infect future partners despite all precautions. They are afraid that they will be rejected when they tell a new partner about their infection. One study by the American Social Health Association (ASHA), an authority on STDs, found that more than

60 percent of people rate herpes as being very traumatic, second only to AIDS.

Common emotional reactions to genital herpes can include anger, depression, isolation, and shame. Some people avoid sexual relationships for a long time, especially if they have once been rejected because of their infection. Some people decide to limit their relationships to other people who have herpes, too. Some people elect not to tell—a choice that often backfires when their partner breaks out with herpes and demands to know where the infection came from.

Proper counseling and medical treatment can make herpes a manageable problem instead of a tragedy. Learning how to tell others of a herpes infection (see Chapter 8), learning to cope with outbreaks, and learning how to lower the risk of infecting future partners can help build confidence and enable one to live a fulfilling life despite a herpes infection.

HOW DOES A DOCTOR DIAGNOSE GENITAL HERPES?

Anyone who thinks they might have genital herpes should be tested as soon as possible. A delay in being tested can make an accurate diagnosis more difficult and increases the risk that others will be infected. Persons who suspect they are infected should stop having sex, especially unprotected sex, until they know how to limit their risk of infecting others.

There are several tests for herpes, and all must be performed by a doctor or health-care expert. The most common and reliable is the lesion culture test in which the doctor takes a swab or scraping of blisters or lesions and sends it to a laboratory to be analyzed. *Antigen* detection tests, performed on material taken from blisters, are also reliable. A positive result means that the herpes virus is present. A negative result may mean that no infection exists, or it may mean that there was no virus in that particular lesion. When test results are negative but symptoms of herpes are present, a follow-up test should be performed. Both culture and antigen detection tests must be performed while a person is having an outbreak.

Diagnosing genital herpes when a person is not having an outbreak involves blood tests and laboratory analysis and has long presented problems for doctors. The ELISA test and the *Western blot immunoassay* test both look for antibodies to the virus in the blood, but ELISA does not distinguish between an HSV-1 and HSV-2 infection, so patients who test positive cannot know whether they have oral or genital herpes. The Western blot test is highly accurate in its results, but is expensive and not widely available.

Several less expensive, newly developed tests promise to make diagnosis of herpes much easier in the future. The Food and Drug Administration (FDA) recently approved at least two procedures that rely on analyzing infected blood. Both are proving to be reliable, rapid, and capable of distinguishing between HSV-1 and 2. "We're very excited about these herpes advances and at the prospects of more people understanding their HSV status," states Linda Alexander, president of ASHA in 1999.

WHAT IS THE TREATMENT FOR GENITAL HERPES?

Treatment for genital herpes is designed to reduce pain and discomfort, shorten the length of outbreaks, and suppress their reoccurrence. This is usually done in two ways: with drug therapy and through alternatives to traditional medical care. A doctor should always be consulted to determine the best combination and course of treatment. Because some doctors are not experts in herpes treatment or may not be sympathetic to patients' questions and concerns, a patient may need to be persistent or "shop around" until the right physician is found.

Drug Therapy

In recent years, several prescription antiviral drugs have been proven to shorten the length of herpes outbreaks. These include acyclovir, valacyclovir, and famciclovir. Such medications do not prevent infection or kill the virus. They act by preventing the virus from replicating (reproducing).

Antiviral drugs need to be started within seventy-two hours of the beginning of an outbreak to be most effective. They must be taken for ten days. If babies who are born with herpes are treated immediately after birth with acyclovir, their chances of avoiding the effects of the disease are greatly increased.

During the first year of infection, when outbreaks may be most frequent and severe, antiviral medications can be taken at a slightly lower dosage and for an indefinite length of time to suppress (lessen) flare-ups. If taken suppressively, medication can reduce the number of outbreaks in 80 percent of people, and eliminate symptoms completely in 50 percent.

There are several steps a person can take to ensure that maximum relief is obtained from prescribed medications. They include:

- Keeping blisters and lesions dry, since this will speed healing
- Wearing loose clothing
- Being tested for other health problems that may be weakening the immune system

- Trying a different antiviral medication if the one being used is not providing satisfactory relief
- Making sure the dosage of medicine is correct (check with your doctor)
- Identifying triggers that may bring on an outbreak—stress, fatigue, certain foods, etc.—and avoiding them if possible

Alternative Treatments

Many herpes sufferers claim that alternative approaches to controlling herpes work as well as or better than antiviral medication. However, some alternative remedies are expensive, some have not been proven safe, and many are not effective for most people. The following, used in conjunction with antiviral medications, may be beneficial and should not be harmful.

Stress Reduction Techniques. Stress may bring on a herpes outbreak, although there is no proof that such is the case. Outbreaks can certainly increase stress and make coping with symptoms more difficult, however. One or more of the following can reduce stress, improve a sufferer's well-being, and help him or her deal with the emotional aspect of having herpes: counseling, regular exercise, relaxation exercises, meditation, biofeedback, or participation in herpes support groups.

Acupuncture. Some sufferers maintain that this therapy decreases the pain associated with outbreaks. There are no studies to prove that acupuncture reduces the frequency of herpes outbreaks, however.

Nutrition and supplements. Experts have proved that a nutritious diet helps support a strong immune system, which can help lessen herpes outbreaks. Some people believe that taking vitamin C, vitamin E, and zinc may boost the immune system. Herpes sufferers who determine that certain foods trigger herpes outbreaks should avoid those foods.

Tea. Many people have found that damp black or green tea bags, placed on herpes sores, can be soothing. Some people believe that drinking green tea can inhibit the virus. Soaking in a warm bath in which several tea bags have been steeped can be both relaxing and pain reducing to herpes sufferers as well.

Drying agents. Substances such as cornstarch and rubbing alcohol that dry out the skin may promote healing of herpes lesions. Alcohol will sting when applied, however.

> Topical corticosteroid creams, commonly used to reduce itching, should never be used to treat herpes. They can make the infection worse.

Ice. Cold compresses or ice, wrapped in a thin towel and applied directly to blisters or lesions, may lessen the severity of symptoms. Some people believe that ice may prevent an outbreak if it is applied during the prodromal warning period.

Herpes can be a painful, unpredictable nuisance or a silent agent that never shows itself. AIDS, the STD described in the next chapter, is much more menacing and disruptive than herpes could ever be, and its threat to teens is very real. The CDC stated in a 1999 report: "It is estimated that at least half of all new HIV infections in the United States are among people under twenty-five, and the majority of young people are infected sexually."

With the risk so high, it pays for teens to know the facts about HIV and AIDS. A rundown of symptoms, diagnosis, and the latest available treatments is given in the next chapter.

Chapter Five

WHAT YOU SHOULD KNOW ABOUT HIV/AIDS

NATHAN

Nathan dropped out of high school when he was sixteen. Classes were hard. Friends were boring. His mother was always nagging him to stop smoking, make better grades, and get a job. Two months later Nathan left home, preferring to live on the streets rather than put up with her criticisms. For two years he survived by panhandling (begging) and prostitution. At night he and several of his street friends gathered in an abandoned building to do drugs, share food, and sleep. "I wasn't happy anywhere in those days," Nathan remembers, "but I was doing what I wanted to do. It was scary at times, but I guess I never thought much about death. I took drugs, shared needles, had sex all over the place, and never worried about the consequences."

One night the odds caught up with Nathan. He was beaten up by a male client and spent several days in the hospital. Among the many tests he underwent was a blood test for HIV. Nathan tested positive. "I had gon-orrhea last year," he states. "I went to a clinic and got treated for that. I didn't bother with anything else. I think a nurse suggested I should be tested for AIDS, but I didn't want to bother."

Nathan knew that he had contracted HIV one of two ways—from having unprotected sex with many partners or from sharing infected needles while doing drugs. When he was released from the hospital he went back to the streets, but his attitude was changing. "I didn't feel invincible anymore. And the HIV thing kind of cramped my style. You know, if you give someone HIV without telling them you're infected, they can come after you for manslaughter or something like that. So I stopped working the streets altogether and started doing some janitor work for a guy I knew."

Then, within one week, two of Nathan's friends died of drug overdoses. "I guess I was more shaken up than I thought," he says. "Suddenly, I just really wanted to go home." Nathan's mother welcomed him back, although she and her son still disagreed on many issues. They managed to overlook their differences, however, and last fall, Nathan enrolled in community college and began working to earn his general equivalency diploma.

Nathan still feels healthy, although he is on a heavy regimen of pills and sees the doctor regularly. He has a positive attitude, and rejects the notion that he will probably develop AIDS and die before he reaches middle age. "I think I'll probably be around to see a cure for HIV," he says confidently.

WHAT IS AIDS?

AIDS (acquired immune deficiency syndrome) is the most complex of all STDs. It is caused by the human immunodeficiency virus (HIV), a *retrovirus* that destroys the immune system—the body's natural ability to fight disease—and leaves a person open to infection and illness. Retroviruses are a family of viruses characterized by a unique mode of replication (reproduction).

The *immune system* fights disease in several ways. It produces white blood cells, known as *lymphocytes*, some of which engulf and destroy worn-out cells, cancer cells, and disease-causing agents (*pathogens*) like

> Your behavior, more than your ethnicity, social status, age, or sexual preference, determines your risk of catching HIV.

bacteria, fungi, and viruses. Some lymphocytes react to invading foreign bodies by forming *antibodies*, which attach to the invaders, inactivate them, and mark them for destruction.

When HIV invades the body, it targets two other types of lymphocytes, the T-helper and T-suppressor cells, which regulate the immune system by controlling the strength and quality of all immune responses. HIV inserts its genetic material into the T cells, replicates inside the cells, and eventually destroys the cells as it goes on to infect others. When HIV first infects the body, a large amount of virus circulates in the system and the number of T cells goes down.

The body's immune system is usually strong enough to suppress the virus for a time. At some point, however, the virus gains the upper hand and numbers of T cells start dropping significantly. It is at this point that a person's immunity becomes seriously impaired, he is considered to have AIDS, and is at high risk of developing a variety of infections and diseases that inevitably prove fatal.

As of the end of 1999, more than 700,000 AIDS cases had been reported to CDC in the United States, and almost 34 million people were infected worldwide. More than 16 million people—at least 3.5 million children under the age of fifteen—have died of AIDS worldwide since the beginning of the epidemic in 1981.

At first, AIDS was predominantly seen as a disease of gay men, but by the late 1990s, a rapid rise in infection rates was seen in heterosexuals who shared drug injection paraphernalia. Today, women and teenagers are two growing at-risk groups. Among teens, females make up almost two thirds of new HIV cases.

Persons who are infected with STDs that cause sores or rashes are at greater risk for catching HIV than those who are not, since the virus passes through breaks in the skin. Women who use oral contraceptives may also be at higher risk, because changes in tissues of the cervix make cells more vulnerable to HIV infection.

HOW IS HIV TRANSMITTED?

HIV can be spread in three ways—sexual transmission, contact with infected blood, and transmission from mother to child.

Sexual transmission includes unprotected vaginal or anal intercourse, oral-genital sex, or other genital contact where semen or vaginal fluids are passed. The risk of becoming infected after one instance of anal or genital contact is somewhere between 1 in 10 and 1 in 300, depending on the virus level in the infected partner's system.

Transmission by contact with infected blood can take place in the following ways:

- Transfusions in which a person receives infected blood or blood product. Today, the risk of infection from blood is very low, since supplies are carefully screened for HIV.

- A stick with a needle that has infected blood on it. Health-care workers are at risk for infection in this manner, but their risk depends on how much virus is present on the needle and on how long ago the needle was used. A person involved in this type of incident usually has a very low risk of becoming infected with HIV.

- An exchange of needles or other infected paraphernalia related to intravenous drug abuse (the abuse of injectable drugs). Persons who use intravenous drugs such as heroin, methamphetamines, and the like, and those who share needles, run a high risk of becoming infected with HIV.

- Contamination with infected blood on mucous membranes or through a break in the skin. Such contamination could possibly occur through acts such as "French" (open mouth) kissing, or through a sharing of razors or toothbrushes, because of the possibility of contact with blood or open sores. The risk depends on how much virus is present and the size of the break in the skin, and appears to be extremely low in most cases.

Transmission from mother to fetus during pregnancy, and from mother to baby during childbirth or breastfeeding are additional means by which HIV can be spread. A baby born to an HIV-positive mother has at least a 12–13 percent chance of being infected at birth. The risk is about 30 percent if the mother is newly infected or has full-blown AIDS. Drug therapy given to an infected mother during pregnancy can significantly decrease a baby's chance of becoming infected. HIV testing is not mandatory, however, so many pregnant women do not know they are infected.

> You cannot catch HIV by giving blood. Blood banks use a new, sterile needle for each individual donor.

Despite widespread fears, HIV does not seem to be transmitted in the following ways:

- Sneezing, coughing, or breathing on food
- Casual contact such as hugging, shaking hands, using public toilets, touching doorknobs, sharing drinking fountains, etc.
- Contact with urine, feces, sputum, sweat, or nasal secretions (unless blood is clearly visible)
- Insect or animal bites
- Sharing work or home environments
- Donating blood

WHAT ARE THE SYMPTOMS OF HIV AND AIDS?

HIV often does not produce symptoms immediately after infection, although a newly infected person is highly contagious. If symptoms do occur, they can be mistaken for flu and can include sore throat, fatigue, fever, headache and muscle aches, nausea and lack of appetite, swollen glands, and a rash over the entire body. Symptoms disappear after one to four weeks, and a person may not realize that he or she has been infected with HIV. "It would be a lost cause trying to remember if I ever felt bad sometime in the past two years," Nathan says. "Living on the street doesn't lead you to feel great anytime."

A period without symptoms follows initial HIV infection. This period may last up to ten years. Individuals are not as infectious during this time as they are in the beginning or when AIDS develops, but they should remember that they are contagious nevertheless.

When symptoms reappear—the onset of AIDS— they include fatigue, shortness of breath, general discomfort, "night sweats," persistent fever, swollen lymph nodes, diarrhea, and unexplained weight loss. Unlike earlier symptoms, these are usually severe enough so that an individual will seek treatment. The body's weakened immune system also allows a variety of mild infections such as thrush (a fungal mouth infection) and vaginal yeast infections to develop. At this stage, infected persons are very contagious due to high levels of virus in the blood.

As AIDS progresses, infected individuals get sick with various *opportunistic infections*, conditions that normally are not life threatening, but can become deadly when a host has low immunity. These can include *Pneumocystis carinii* pneumonia, toxoplasmosis (a parasitic infection), tuberculosis, severe herpes infections, fungal infections, Kaposi's sarcoma (a rare, aggressive form of cancer), and non-Hodgkin's lymphoma (cancer of the lymph system). Women with AIDS have a higher occurrence of cervical cancer than do uninfected women. They are also more likely than men to have oral fungal infections, bacterial pneumonia infections, and progressive multifocal leukencephalopathy (PML), a viral infection of the central nervous system.

As the immune system continues to weaken, illnesses become more frequent and more severe.

Eventually, sufferers are unable to recover from the many illnesses that attack the body. They become thin, weak, and cannot perform the ordinary functions of everyday life. Death from AIDS is often a slow, painful, and traumatic experience both for the sufferers and for those who love and care for them.

Children who are infected with HIV generally develop AIDS much more quickly than do adults, and the progress of their disease tends to be more rapid. Many children who are born with HIV do not live more than two years. Symptoms of AIDS in children include most of those that afflict adults, but children also suffer from more bacterial, viral, and fungal infections than do adults. HIV infection can slow the growth of children and impair their intellectual development and coordination.

WHAT SHOULD I KNOW BEFORE I GET TESTED FOR HIV INFECTION?

Deciding to be tested for HIV infection is difficult for most people. Receiving a positive diagnosis can be a devastating experience. Persons who choose to be tested sometimes consider taking a close friend along for moral support. Some also find it helpful to look into the availability of counselors to turn to if the news is bad.

Anyone who is thinking about being tested for HIV/AIDS should also consider the issue of confidentiality. Normally, medical procedures carried out by a doctor or a clinic are confidential—that is, they are part of a person's medical record and can be released only with his or her written permission. However, if information leaks, and outsiders such as employers access this information, a patient may be labeled "high risk." The patient may lose his or her job or have difficulty getting insurance coverage for treatment in the future.

Because of the risk of discrimination that still haunts persons with HIV/AIDS, some people choose to take an anonymous diagnostic test that allows them to identify themselves only by a first name or a number. With an anonymous test, only the patient receives the results of the procedure. This test can be performed as an in-clinic procedure or utilizing an at-home kit. There is some danger from using at-home kits, however, since they can be performed improperly and can give unreliable results.

HOW DOES A DOCTOR DIAGNOSE HIV/AIDS?

Diagnosing HIV. HIV infection can be diagnosed by testing for the presence of antibodies in the blood or saliva using the ELISA test. Because it takes time for antibodies to be produced by the body, however, a reliable diagnosis cannot be made until three to six months after possible infection. To confirm a positive ELISA test, antibodies must also be detected by the Western blot immunoassay test. Both tests are highly accurate, and, when used in combination, identify most cases of HIV infection.

> If your doctor does not take the time to listen to your concerns, you should consider finding another health-care provider who better fits your needs.

The p24 antigen test detects early infection more quickly than antibody tests do and is often used by blood banks to screen out infected blood. It is also used to detect infection in babies born to HIV-infected mothers. All such babies are born with HIV antibodies circulating in their blood and thus test positive to the

69

ELISA and the Western blot immunoassay tests whether infected or not.

Diagnosing AIDS. For a diagnosis of AIDS to be made, a person's T-helper cell count must fall below 200 cells per cubic millimeter of blood. (The normal level of T-helper cells in the blood is about 1,000 per cubic millimeter.) The presence of at least one of twenty-six indicator infections such as *Pneumocystis carinii* pneumonia, toxoplasmosis, pulmonary tuberculosis, or invasive cervical cancer can also be grounds for a positive diagnosis of AIDS if there is no other reason for immune system damage.

WHAT IS THE TREATMENT FOR HIV/AIDS?

AIDS is likely to remain incurable for some time to come, but there have been promising developments in the control and suppression of HIV infection since the 1980s. Drug therapy, counseling, and alternatives to traditional medicine can and do prove helpful to those who seek the best course of treatment. With such treatment, AIDS patients are now able to live relatively healthy lives for years after the onset of the disease.

> A person does not die of AIDS, but of complications that stem from the many opportunistic infections or cancers an AIDS patient develops.

Drug Therapy
Management of HIV and AIDS is a complicated process and involves many visits to the doctor or health-care facility. Individual medication plans must be set up and managed. Regular blood tests are necessary to monitor levels of T-helper cells and to see if medications are effectively suppressing the virus. Opportunistic infec-

tions must be treated and controlled to lower the risk of fatal complications. Because of such complexities, treatment can be virtually a never-ending task.

There are no drugs currently available that kill HIV, but three classes of HIV-suppressive drugs—*nucleoside analogues, non-nucleoside reverse transcriptase inhibitors* (NNRTIs), and *protease inhibitors*—are commonly used to prolong the life and health of an infected person. Nucleoside analogues include AZT (azidothymidine), didanosine, zalcitabine, and stavudine, all of which are not particularly powerful when used alone and commonly are effective for a relatively short period of time. NNRTIs are most effective when used in combination with nucleoside analogues. They include nevirapine, delavirdine, and efavirenz. Protease inhibitors, first approved in 1995, are more powerful than nucleosides and NNRTIs and include ritonavir, indinavir, nelfinavir, and amprenavir.

Experts have found that combination therapy works best in treating HIV. For instance, they might prescribe a protease inhibitor and two nucleoside analogues. When three drugs are combined, HIV levels in the blood can be reduced to almost undetectable levels. Daily doses of medication can total up to twenty pills, however, and side effects are often severe. It can also be difficult to remember to take all medications correctly. "It's corny, but I have one of those little divided pillboxes that I carry," Nathan explains. "My mom reminds me if she's around and notices that I've skipped a dose. It's almost a full-time job remembering." Failure to follow instructions can be disastrous because only a few mistakes can allow HIV to become resistant to drug treatment.

To get the best results from drug therapy, persons with HIV/AIDS are encouraged to adopt a healthy lifestyle. This includes eliminating smoking, drug use, and excessive alcohol consumption. Patients are also encouraged to follow recommendations to protect themselves against other STDs and to protect others from catching HIV. They are instructed to be checked for tuberculosis regularly. HIV-infected women are also urged to have a *Pap smear* every six months to test for cervical cancer.

Counseling
Emotional support is a vital part of HIV/AIDS treatment. Being diagnosed as HIV-positive can be very traumatic. Guidance and counseling from a psychologist, social worker, or health-care worker can make a huge difference in how one deals with emotional distress, maintains a sense of hope and purpose, and continues to live a productive life.

A variety of groups—self-help, support, stress management, and grief management—exist that can help infected individuals deal with the depression, despair, and social rejection that can be a part of living with HIV and AIDS. Counseling centers and churches also provide support and individual or group counseling. Family counseling can help parents or siblings who are distressed by the diagnosis of HIV in another family member. Refer to the Resources section at the end of this book to locate support organizations in your region.

Alternative Treatments
Many people who have HIV and AIDS choose to combine traditional drug treatment and counseling with alternative treatments that can include herbal therapy, acupuncture, vitamins, and changes in diet. Books are available on the topic, and practitioners of alternative medicine can provide advice and guidance. Before beginning such treatments, a physician should be con-

sulted to ensure that no harmful effects will result. Alternative therapies should supplement, not take the place of, drug therapy when it comes to AIDS treatment.

WHAT IS THE COST OF TREATMENT?

The cost of treatment for AIDS can be extremely high, and after a number of years of treatment, totals can grow unmanageably large. People in developing countries are often unable to afford the most effective therapies that are now available. In the United States, government programs such the AIDS Drug Assistance Program (ADAP) help pay for costly medications for those who have limited finances or do not have private insurance.

Financial questions are not foremost in the minds of most teens when they think of AIDS. To them, the most compelling concern is that HIV is a killer—the top infectious disease in the world.

Other STDs pose very serious threats to young people's health as well. Two lesser-known infections—*human papillomavirus* (HPV) and hepatitis B—are widespread and can be almost as dangerous as AIDS. "The incidence of HPV infection in sexually active young college women is alarming," says Penny Hitchcock, an expert in STDs with the National Institute of Allergy and Infectious Disease (NIAID). "Furthermore, we currently have no effective way to prevent infection."

Information about HPV, hepatitis B, and the problems they cause is included in the following chapter.

Chapter Six

WHAT YOU SHOULD KNOW ABOUT GENITAL WARTS AND HEPATITIS B

MIGUEL AND LARISSA

Miguel, a senior in high school, thinks that his girl-friend, Larissa, is the most beautiful girl in his class. He may be right. Larissa has done some modeling for a local agency, and hopes to go to New York to see if she might have a chance of signing on with one of the big agencies there. "I'd like to think we'll be together forever," Miguel says, "but Larissa has big plans."

From the beginning, Miguel and Larissa's relationship has been physical, although they have not yet had sexual intercourse. Miguel has been intimate with other girlfriends in the past, but this time, some worrisome bumps on his penis, bumps that were never there before, have caused him to hesitate. "I told myself they were nothing, but they kept getting bigger," he says. "Finally I went to the doctor."

Miguel looked in the phone book and made an appointment with a clinic in a nearby town where he could have his problem checked. At the clinic Miguel learned that he has genital warts, an STD that is fairly common among teens. "I asked the doctor for some medicine to get rid of them, and he said there was no cure. He also said they were really contagious. I freaked. It was the worst day of my life."

For a while Miguel thought about breaking up with Larissa. He was embarrassed by his problem, and he felt bad at the thought that he could infect her. Larissa was flatteringly eager to be with him, however, and it seemed too hard to tell her about his condition. One weekend when her parents were away, she invited Miguel over to her home, and they went "all the way." Miguel offered to use a condom, but Larissa told him she was on the Pill, so he let the issue slide.

Now Miguel has an uncomfortable feeling that maybe he ought to have said something to Larissa about his infection. They have been sexually intimate for a month, and he still can't find the right words. "So far, nothing bad has happened," he says. "I kind of wish she wanted to be a little more careful, but I guess that's up to her. Maybe it'll all work out in the end."

WHAT ARE GENITAL WARTS?

Despite Miguel's wishful thinking, if he continues to have unprotected sex with Larissa, she will probably catch genital warts (also known as venereal warts), one of the most common STDs in the United States today. Genital warts are caused by the human papillomavirus (HPV), a family of more than seventy different types of viruses that cause warts on hands, feet, and genitals. Most people are infected with some type of HPV, although they may not have warts of any kind. About one third of all types of human papillomavirus cause genital warts. The type of HPV that produces genital warts does not commonly cause warts on hands and feet, and vice versa.

About one half of all sexually active adults are infected with a type of HPV that causes genital warts, and the incidence of infection appears to be on the increase. An estimated one million new cases are diagnosed every year in the United States. The chances of getting HPV through a sexual encounter with an infected person are high. About two thirds of people who have repeated sexual contact with someone infected with genital warts will become infected within three months. The more partners a person has, the greater the chances of becoming infected with HPV.

Genital warts are very common among young people. Some studies show that one third of all sexually active teens have genital HPV infections. Young women, particularly those who become sexually active before the age of eighteen, have a high risk of contracting genital HPV, since the cervix is not fully mature and can be easily infected. The risk to men is significant as well. Between 60 and 90 percent of men whose partners are infected also have HPV.

According to some experts, smoking may increase a person's risk for developing genital warts because it suppresses the immune system, allowing HPV more chance to manifest itself. In one study of almost six hundred women, smokers were five times as likely to develop visible warts as were nonsmokers.

HOW IS HPV TRANSMITTED?

HPV lives in the skin and is transmitted through skin-to-skin contact during vaginal, anal, or oral-genital sex. HPV is not passed through blood, semen, or other body fluids. A person can be infectious even if no symptoms are present, but the risk is probably greatest if contact is made with the warts themselves. The thin mucous membranes of the vagina, vulva, penis, and scrotum are particularly prone to infection.

Babies can sometimes become infected with HPV at birth while passing through the vagina of infected mothers. There is little or no risk of catching HPV from towels or other inanimate objects.

WHAT ARE THE SYMPTOMS OF HUMAN PAPILLOMAVIRUS?

Most people who are infected with the human papillomavirus have no symptoms at all. Visible symptoms are small bumps (warts), which usually develop between thirty and ninety days after initial infection. In a few people, warts may not appear until years after the initial infection.

With genital types of HPV, warts develop on the penis and scrotum, inside the urethra, around and inside the vagina, and on the cervix of the uterus. They may appear inside and around the anus, on the lower abdomen and upper thighs, and in the groin. Occasionally they occur in the mouth and throat, or on the lips, eyelids, and nipples. A person may never know he or she has genital warts if this condition occurs only inside the urethra or on the vagina or cervix.

Genital warts can look like regular warts. They may be flesh colored or darker, and they are usually harder than surrounding tissue. They may be flat or raised, single or multiple, large or small. They can grow and spread and assume a cauliflower-like appearance, or they may remain small and barely noticeable. They may itch, but they usually do not hurt unless they are scratched and become irritated.

77

Often genital warts go away without treatment. The virus does not disappear, however. It remains in the body indefinitely, and when it reactivates, new outbreaks of warts can occur. People can experience outbreaks of genital warts throughout their lifetime, although the virus commonly becomes less active as time passes.

ARE THERE COMPLICATIONS FROM HPV?

Most genital warts are harmless, but they can have dangerous consequences because they increase a person's chances of developing cancer in the genital area, particularly cancer of the penis, anus, vulva, and cervix.

> Cervical cancer is curable 90 percent of the time if it is detected and treated in its early stages.

Cervical cancer is a particular concern with genital HPV. According to the American Cancer Society, about 13,000 women develop cervical cancer every year, and about 4,600 die. Certain types of HPV have been found to be responsible for cellular changes that can lead to cervical cancer, and when cervical cancer lesions are examined under a microscope, HPV is detected about 90 percent of the time. Women who have HPV, therefore, must be doubly sure to get a regular Pap smear (a test to detect cancerous or precancerous cells of the cervix) every six months in order to detect changes early.

Genital warts not only increase the risk of cancer, they can also cause problems during pregnancy, when they have a tendency to grow rapidly. If they enlarge, they can make urination difficult. If present on the wall of the vagina, they can cause obstruction during delivery. Infants born to infected mothers may develop warts on their larynx (voice box). This is a potentially life-threatening condition that requires frequent laser surgery to keep airways open.

HOW DOES A DOCTOR DIAGNOSE HUMAN PAPILLOMAVIRUS?

Human papillomavirus is almost always diagnosed by the presence of visible warts. There are techniques that can detect the genetic material of the virus, but these are very expensive and not commonly used except in research.

Genital warts need to be diagnosed by an experienced health-care provider. The skin of the genitals can be bumpy and irregular, and a trained eye may be necessary to decide what is normal and what is not. A procedure called a *colposcopy* is sometimes used to detect warts that may not otherwise be easily seen, such as those that grow on the cervix. A Pap smear can reveal abnormalities in cells consistent with HPV infection, but a Pap smear is not an accurate diagnostic tool for HPV or other STDs. A person can have a normal Pap smear and still be infected with HPV or other STDs.

WHAT IS THE TREATMENT FOR GENITAL WARTS?

There is no cure for human papillomavirus. Because most warts are not dangerous, some people choose to live with them and see if they go away on their own. In many cases, genital warts disappear without treatment. If warts are large, irritated and bleeding, or embarrassing, they can be removed.

There are several procedures available for removal of genital warts. A doctor should be consulted to see which procedure is best, depending on the size, number, and location of the growths. Removal procedures include:

- Cryotherapy—freezing warts off with liquid nitrogen
- Physician-applied medications such as podophyllin and trichloracetic acid, or prescription medications such as imiquimod cream, applied directly to the surface of the warts
- Electrocautery (burning) or laser therapy
- Surgical removal
- Alpha interferon treatment—used when warts recur after removal by other means

> Do NOT attempt to remove genital warts with over-the-counter wart removal preparations. See your doctor instead.

All of these treatments can eliminate warts and perhaps lower the risk of transmitting the virus to others. Removal does not guarantee that warts will not return, however. Most people who have genital warts removed will experience recurrences.

WHAT IS HEPATITIS B?

While human papillomavirus increases a person's risk of various genital cancers, hepatitis B attacks the liver and can cause severe illness and even death.

Hepatitis B is one of a family of hepatitis viruses. Unlike hepatitis A, which is spread through contaminated food and water, hepatitis B is commonly passed through an exchange of infected body fluids including blood, semen, vaginal secretions, fluid from wounds, and saliva. Hepatitis C is also a blood-borne strain that can cause severe liver damage and death, but it seems rarely to be passed through normal sexual contact.

Hepatitis B virus is a highly transmissible disease, about one hundred times more contagious than the AIDS virus. It can survive outside of the body for at least seven days on a dry surface. Although a vaccine is lowering the rate of infection, in the late 1990s about 200,000 Americans were infected annually, and about 5,000 Americans died each year of complications from hepatitis B.

Those people at highest risk of catching hepatitis B are individuals who have unprotected sex with more than one partner, men who have sex with men, people who live with someone who has chronic hepatitis B, people who have jobs that involve contact with human blood, and people who travel to regions where hepatitis B is common—Southeast Asia, Africa, the Amazon Basin, the Pacific Islands, and the Middle East. Teens whose parents were born in those regions are doubly at risk because a parent with chronic hepatitis B may pass the disease to them by nonsexual means. In the late 1990s, about 70 percent of new cases of hepatitis B occurred among people age fifteen to thirty-nine. Of that total, 75 percent were teenagers.

HOW IS HEPATITIS B TRANSMITTED?

Hepatitis B is commonly passed from person to person through unprotected sexual contact including vaginal, anal, and oral sex. Many people catch hepatitis B while sharing drug paraphernalia with infected friends.

Mothers can pass the virus to their unborn children during pregnancy and delivery. Unborn babies whose mothers are infected with hepatitis B have a greater than 80 percent chance of being born with hepatitis.

Other possible means of transmission include:

- Sharing toothbrushes, nail clippers, or razors with an infected person (because of the risk of contact with blood or body fluids).
- Getting tattooed, having acupuncture treatment, or getting one's body pierced with unsterile equipment.
- Receiving contaminated blood through a transfusion. The risk of this is rare today because blood supplies have been routinely screened since 1975.
- Any other activity where there can be a transfer of infected body fluids through the skin, such as with a human bite.
- Kissing or having regular household contact with an infected person.

WHAT ARE THE SYMPTOMS OF HEPATITIS B?

People infected with hepatitis B may have no symptoms, although they will still be infectious. About two thirds of those with hepatitis B antibodies in their blood never recall having the disease.

For those who do show symptoms, these generally appear between one and four months after infection and can be mistaken for the flu. Symptoms then progress and can include:

- Achy joints
- Extreme tiredness and loss of appetite

- Mild fever
- Abdominal pain
- Diarrhea and light-colored bowel movements
- Nausea and vomiting
- Jaundice (yellowing of the skin and the whites of the eyes)
- Dark urine

Symptoms range from mild to severe and usually last about one to two months. A few patients experience liver failure and death shortly after infection. About 90–95 percent of people who are infected recover completely and then have lifelong immunity from becoming infected again. (They can, however, become infected with different strains of hepatitis.)

About 5–10 percent of infected individuals do not recover within six months and are considered chronically infected. (Babies who are born infected are at risk of becoming chronically infected as well.) About one million Americans are chronically infected with hepatitis B at the present.

One third of people who are chronically infected go on to develop chronic active hepatitis, which can lead to serious damage of the liver (cirrhosis), liver cancer,

> Every week, hundreds of teenagers are infected with hepatitis B.

and death. Two thirds of those who are chronically infected have chronic persistent hepatitis and suffer mild inflammation of the liver. They are still at some risk of developing cirrhosis and liver cancer, but their risk is not as great.

Chronically infected individuals are also *carriers* of the disease—that is, they are contagious even though they show no outward symptoms of the virus. Although chronically infected individuals are commonly infected for the rest of their lives, they can and do spontaneously recover at times.

HOW DOES A DOCTOR DIAGNOSE HEPATITIS B?

Physical symptoms and abnormal liver function tests are the first clues to a doctor that a person may be infected with hepatitis. Specific blood tests that look for antibodies or virus antigens are necessary to confirm a diagnosis, however. In rare cases of chronic hepatitis, it may be necessary to perform a liver biopsy, a procedure that involves examining a small sample of liver tissue under a microscope. This can determine the stage of infection and the extent of damage that has been done.

Anyone who is found to be infected with hepatitis B should also be tested for hepatitis D (delta hepatitis), a blood-borne strain that can also cause severe liver damage. Hepatitis D uses hepatitis B to reproduce and survive, and thus only infects people who have hepatitis B. Hepatitis D is transmitted through the sharing of infected needles and through sexual contact.

WHAT IS THE TREATMENT FOR HEPATITIS B?

There is no cure for hepatitis B, but in most cases, the infection goes away on its own. During the period when symptoms are present, doctors usually prescribe bed rest and plenty of fluids. Hospitalization is not necessary unless a person has other medical problems or is extremely ill.

People with chronic hepatitis infections sometimes benefit from treatment with alpha interferon, an antiviral protein produced by white blood cells. Interferon is not well understood, but it plays a role in the body's defense against viruses, bacteria, and other disease-causing agents. The drug lamivudine is also used in some cases, but viral resistance to treatment may occur. Alpha interferon and lamivudine should not be used together.

People with liver failure as a result of hepatitis B can have their lives extended by a liver transplant, but reinfection of the new liver is a possibility.

A VACCINE FOR HEPATITIS B

Hepatitis B may be incurable, but it is also totally preventable. A safe and effective vaccine—three shots over the course of six months—became available in 1982, eliminating the risk of infection for those who are immunized (take the vaccine).

Immunization against hepatitis B is also protection against hepatitis D.

The CDC recommends that all babies be vaccinated against hepatitis B at birth. Others who should be vaccinated include:

- Teens who have not been vaccinated, particularly teens who are sexually active or who practice tattooing or body piercing
- Teens whose parents come from Southeast Asia, Africa, the Amazon Basin, the Pacific Islands, and the Middle East
- People who use drugs
- People whose jobs expose them to human blood
- People who are partners of or live with someone with hepatitis B

Anyone who is exposed to hepatitis B, but who has not been immunized, can be given the vaccination series plus a dose of immune globulin, a collection of antibodies that boosts the immune system for a short time. The two together offer some protection against becoming infected. Children who are born to infected mothers stand a good chance of not becoming infected if they receive vaccine plus immune globulin within twelve hours after birth.

Researchers are working hard to develop vaccines that will prevent other STDs such as gonorrhea, herpes, AIDS, and genital warts. Except for hepatitis B, however, none are on the market, and it may be some time before they become available. Until they are, teens need to be smart and responsible and know how to respond when risky situations arise. In Chapter Seven, information is presented to help young people determine their sexual boundaries, communicate effectively with partners, and prevent infection with an STD.

HOW YOU CAN AVOID CATCHING AN STD

- Do you know you can virtually eliminate your risk of catching an STD?
- Do you know that a condom greatly reduces your chances of contracting an STD?
- Do you know that birth-control pills prevent pregnancy, but not STDs?
- Do you know that you should plan ahead so you can talk to your boyfriend or girlfriend about STDs before you decide to have sex?

Sexually transmitted diseases range from annoying and painful ailments to life-changing, life-threatening illnesses. Protecting oneself from them is more than just a good idea. It is an investment in future good health, in future relationships, in the ability to have children, perhaps in the chance for a long life.

Too many young people choose to ignore STDs, however. Even faced with the risk of AIDS, many teens in the United States have sex with people they scarcely know and have sexual encounters while using alcohol and drugs. In studies of high school and college students, only about half of those who are sexually active use condoms every time they have sex, and nearly half report that they have had more than one partner. Some teens say they have had seven or more partners.

Having casual sex is very risky business. There is no protection in attending a good school, coming from a good family, and living in a middle class suburban neighborhood. The pretty girl sitting across the aisle in math class could be infected with chlamydia, just as the boy next door might have genital herpes or HIV. Teens who tell themselves that it's okay to be careless and irresponsible just once could be making a deadly mistake. Fortunately, anyone can lower if not eliminate the risk of catching an STD by making some changes in his or her sexual behavior.

CELESTE

Celeste's STD infection is a thing of the past, but she still feels embarrassed every time she sees Kurtis at school. She wonders if the authorities notified him of his STD, and if he knows that they found out because of her. "I feel like a snitch," she says, "which is stupid, because it wasn't my fault."

Celeste has decided to learn from her mistake and be very careful not to mix alcohol and physical relationships in the future. She went to the library and checked out a book on STDs, just so she won't feel so ignorant. "I thought only 'bad' people got STDs," she admits. "That's obviously not the case. These are equal opportunity infections."

ABSTINENCE—BE 100 PERCENT SURE

There is only one sure way to prevent catching an STD—total *abstinence*. That means not engaging in vaginal, anal, or oral sex or any other sexual activity that involves genital contact. It means no illegal intravenous drug use and sharing of needles. It may also mean no open-mouth kissing that can involve an exchange of saliva or blood (a mode of transmitting hepatitis B).

Abstinence is not a popular notion with many people today. The media and society make it seem like total abstention from sexual activity is impossible or even psychologically harmful for healthy, well-adjusted human beings. Such is not necessarily the case, however. Abstinence is practiced in many world religions, and prior to the sexual revolution of the 1960s, most people waited until marriage before having sexual intercourse. Today, many teens choose abstinence for a variety of spiritual, emotional, and physical reasons.

Abstinence for teens usually means just postponing sexual activity until they are older, have some life experience, and have found a partner whom they hope to be with for the rest of their life. It means not treating sex casually. It means believing in their own worth and resisting peer pressure to have sex just because everyone else is having it.

"SAFER" SEX

For teens who do not choose abstinence, there are ways to reduce the risk of catching an STD. The first and foremost involves always using a latex (rubber) condom to block the transmission of bacteria and viruses. Many teens use condoms, but not every time they have sex.

Condoms can be purchased in any grocery, drug, or discount store, and no prescription is necessary. Many teens, especially males, object to using condoms, claiming that they are too much trouble, are too embarrassing to buy, or are not perfectly reliable. As a matter of fact, it is worth a little trouble and embarrassment to protect oneself against dangerous STDs like herpes and AIDS. And intimate behavior may actually be more enjoyable when partners are not fearful of becoming pregnant or infected with an STD.

If condoms are used correctly, failure rates are only about 2 percent. Many condoms that fail have been stored incorrectly or put on improperly. Although condoms do not offer protection from all sores and lesions or from viral shedding, they do significantly lower the risk of catching an STD. If a person follows instructions for storage and usage that are included in the package, condoms can be up to 10,000 times safer than having unprotected sex.

In 1993 the Food and Drug Administration approved the first female condom, trade-named Reality. The device is the first barrier contraceptive for women that provides protection against STDs. It consists of a polyurethane sheath with a flexible ring on each end. The inner ring and sheath is inserted in the vagina. The outer ring and a portion of the sheath remains outside the body, partially covering the labia. Questions about the effectiveness of female condoms in preventing pregnancy and protecting against STDs remain. Female condoms are also more expensive than male condoms. However, they have one important plus. "It definitely gives women some control," states one of the product's promoters. "If the man won't wear one, the woman can."

NAKEESHA AND SERGIO

Because Nakeesha wants to continue her relationship with Sergio, she finally worked up her courage and talked to him about the behavior that put her and their baby at risk for serious health problems. "Sergio claims he's been true to me—that he must have got chlamydia before we met," she says. "I guess I believe him, but I told him he has to wear a condom every time we have sex, at least until after the baby is born. And I'm going to get regular checkups for STDs for a while. I have to be healthy for my children—they're my first priority right now."

GUIDELINES TO LOWER YOUR RISK

There are other steps Nakeesha and other teens can take to reduce the risk of catching or transmitting an STD. They include:

- Limiting the number of sexual partners one has and choosing partners carefully.
- Never having any kind of sex with someone whose health and sexual practices are unknown. This includes avoiding all genital contact as well.
- If a partner's sexual history is unknown, avoiding any activity that puts one in contact with that partner's semen, blood, or other body fluids. This can include deep or open-mouth kissing.
- Talking with a partner about past sexual experiences before having sex. This means knowing that person well enough to be comfortable talking about intimate matters. Be aware that not everyone is honest about their past.

- Never having sex while under the influence of drugs or alcohol.
- Never sharing needles or having sex with an intravenous drug user who shares needles.
- Knowing the visible signs and symptoms of STDs. A person should never have sex or be intimate if a partner has signs of infection.
- Using a new condom for each act of sexual intercourse.
- Never using natural condoms, called "skins" or "lambskins." They are more porous than latex condoms and can allow HIV and other viruses to slip though. Only water-based lubricants such as K-Y jelly, Astroglide, Aqua-lube and glycerin should be used. Oil-based lubricants such as Vaseline, shortening, mineral oil, massage oil, body lotions, and cooking oil can damage latex condoms.
- Never relying on spermicides containing the ingredient nonoxynol-9 to take the place of a condom. Nonoxynol-9, believed by some to kill STD microbes, is not adequate protection against STDs and may even increase the risk of HIV transmission.
- When deciding to have sex, planning ahead to make it as safe as possible. This includes thinking through what to say if an unexpected situation comes up, for instance if a partner shows symptoms of an STD.
- Carrying a condom if there is the slightest risk of having sex, and insisting that one be used for every sexual encounter. Every teen should be prepared to refuse to have sex if a partner refuses to use a condom.

- Getting vaccinated for hepatitis B.
- Going to a doctor or an STD clinic immediately after possible exposure to an STD. Everyone who has multiple sex partners should be checked for STDs by a doctor or health-care provider every six months.

WHO SHOULD BE TESTED FOR STDS?

Teens who are sexually active and meet any of the following criteria should talk to a health-care provider about being tested for STDs:

- Had unprotected sex with a partner and don't know if he or she is infected
- Had a new sexual partner within the past sixty days
- Had more than two sexual partners in the past six months
- Had sexual contact with someone with an STD or have been infected with an STD in the past twelve months
- Are pregnant or planning to become pregnant
- Are not consistently using a condom for birth and infection control with new partners
- Have been diagnosed with pelvic inflammatory disease or infections of the urethra, epididymis, or prostate

DARE TO BE EXCEPTIONAL

Avoiding STDs can seem like an extremely complicated process, one that involves discipline and restraint that even many adults seem to lack today. Most teens have a multitude of other things to think about, too. They don't want to spend a minute concentrating on something as unpleasant and problematic as a sexually transmitted disease. For those who do, just thinking about buying condoms makes many feel tremendously guilty and embarrassed. Trying to decide how to ask a date about his or her sexual history is mind-boggling to contemplate.

Carelessness when it comes to sex can be deadly, however. Smart teens need to know their options and decide what they think. They can get information and advice from a variety of sources. They can talk to someone who is knowledgeable and nonjudgmental—a family member, teacher, or family doctor—about questions relating to sex and sexual relationships. They can learn about STDs from a sex education class in school or from a health provider at an STD clinic. For teens who are nervous about approaching adults, some schools and communities have programs staffed by trained teen volunteers. And there are always library books like this one. "I was so embarrassed I fibbed and told the librarian I was doing a report for health class when I checked out a book on STDs," says Celeste. "The librarian was really nice and suggested I look for information on the Internet, too."

Teens should never try to fool themselves into believing that they cannot catch an STD. The smartest face facts and acknowledge that they could indeed get chlamydia, herpes, or AIDS if they have sex, especially unprotected sex, with the wrong person. After facing that fact, they then have to ask themselves—do I want to take chances with my health, or am I going to behave wisely and responsibly in any sexual relationships I may choose to have now or in the future?

In some cases, the information necessary to act responsibly, set personal limits, and prevent catching an STD is ignored or comes too late. Teens have unprotected sex, and then discover that they're infected with an STD. Sometimes it's one for which there is no cure.

For teens infected with a chronic STD, the thought of having it for the rest of their life can be very disturbing. There is reason to be optimistic, however. With the exception of AIDS, the possibility of living a long and happy life is good. Even with AIDS, teens can control their symptoms and improve their quality of life. Learn more about living with a chronic STD in the next chapter.

Chapter Eight

LIVING WITH A CHRONIC STD

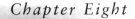

There are several things teens can do if they discover they are infected with a chronic STD like herpes, genital warts, or AIDS. First, they can stop blaming themselves or the person who may have caused the infection. Finding fault won't help. It is far better to focus on doing everything possible to ensure health, happiness, and responsible decision making in the future. That includes being as knowledgeable as possible about STDs, getting necessary treatments, maintaining a healthy lifestyle, and identifying supporters to turn to if and when times get tough.

NATHAN

A short time ago, while helping his mother at a church garage sale, Nathan met Janice, another college student. Janice is aware of Nathan's past and accepts the fact that he has HIV. They like each other, but neither knows if they'll have a long-term relationship. "My mom asked her church for prayer about my HIV, so Janice knew about it from the start," he explains. "After we became friends, she showed me how to get on the Internet and get all this information about AIDS. She's helped me get connected with a support group. It's made me feel less isolated, less like it's just *my* problem."

BE INFORMED

Teens living with a chronic STD are wise to find out everything they can about their disease. For instance, if they have genital herpes, they can learn to recognize the prodromal symptoms that may signal an upcoming outbreak, or pinpoint and avoid foods or situations that trigger outbreaks. Teens with HIV might want to learn about ways to build up their immune system and try to put those into practice. They can ask their doctor about new types of treatments and new medications that come on the market.

Teens should be aware that being infected with an STD that causes blisters or sores puts them at greater risk for catching other STDs. For instance, during a herpes outbreak, a person can more easily contract HIV from an infected partner. Infected teens need to know what to do to be safe during sexual encounters. They need to keep their partners informed of any risks, particularly if they are dealing with HIV.

GET REGULAR MEDICAL CHECKUPS

Regular medical checkups are vital for teens infected with chronic STDs. Prompt detection and diagnosis can lessen the risk of future complications. For instance,

USING A CONDOM

If properly used, condoms can help reduce the risk of passing sexually transmitted diseases. It is necessary to follow a few simple guidelines to achieve the greatest protection.

- Handle a condom gently.
- If a condom feels sticky or stiff or if it does not unroll all the way, throw it away and get a new one.
- Put a condom on before the penis gets anywhere near any body opening to avoid exposure to body fluids that can carry infection.
- For male condoms, apply after the penis is erect. Be sure the rolled-up ring is on the outside. When applying, squeeze the tip of the condom gently so no air is trapped inside. Leave space at the tip to hold semen after ejaculation. Withdraw while penis is still erect to prevent spilling semen.
- For female condoms, carefully follow package instructions. Insert the inner ring as far as it will go, and make sure the outer ring is outside the vagina. Apply lubricant inside the condom or to the penis. Remove condom before standing up.

young women with genital warts should get regular Pap smears to detect cellular changes that can lead to cervical cancer.

A physician can be an excellent source of information about ways to cope with a chronic STD, but it may be up to the patient to bring up specific questions or concerns. Teens who are going to visit a doctor might want to make a list of their concerns, to avoid forgetting or overlooking something while they are in the office.

For those teens who cannot afford to go to a doctor, most communities have health departments, infectious disease clinics, STD clinics, women's health clinics, and/or family-planning clinics where testing and treatment are confidential and low cost. The National STD Hot Line of the CDC, listed in the Resources section of this book, can help access treatment centers in specific locales.

Drugs that are prescribed to treat an STD should be taken as directed. This may mean taking a pill at a certain time of day or avoiding certain foods while taking certain medications. It is important not to skip doses, combine doses, or stop taking medicine too soon. Doctors or health-care providers are always happy to answer patients' questions. Follow-up appointments are also important to ensure that side effects are not serious and that prescribed drugs are working as they should.

ADOPT A HEALTHY LIFESTYLE

A strong immune system is a person's best defense against outbreaks of herpes or the progression of AIDS. Maintaining a healthy lifestyle will help keep the immune system strong. Some factors that make up a healthy lifestyle include:

- Eating right. The USDA Food Pyramid, which places emphasis on grains, fruits, and vegetables and calls for the sparing use of fats, is a sensible guide to follow.
- Getting eight hours of sleep a night.
- Avoiding the use of cigarettes and the misuse of alcohol and drugs.
- Exercising regularly.
- Reducing stress.

FIND SOMEONE TO TALK TO

Young people who learn that they have an STD may feel terrified, overwhelmed, and deeply depressed, especially if they have been diagnosed with HIV. Because STDs are linked with promiscuity, prostitution, drug abuse, and homosexuality, teens may feel a deep sense of shame when they find that they are infected. Some teens may even decide to keep the news a secret from everyone, including their parents and their closest friends.

It is normal to experience a variety of negative feelings when bad news strikes, but no one should try to cope with such feelings alone. Family and friends are often a young person's strongest supporters and can provide valuable guidance and encouragement during traumatic times. Many teens fear and put off telling parents, convinced that they will be judgmental, harsh, and unreasonable. In most cases, this is not true, although most parents will need time to assimilate the news and react to it. Parents may be initially shocked and dismayed, but most are committed to loving and helping their children through good times and bad. The majority will be understanding of mistakes and willing to do what they can to help their children adjust to the ramifications of an illness. "My mom cried when I told her I was HIV positive, but she never said, 'I told you so.' She never makes me feel guilty," says Nathan.

If parents and family are not available or supportive, or if additional assistance is needed, religious leaders, health-care workers, and counselors are always willing to provide comfort, insights, and encouragement. Teen volunteers who staff hot lines and/or community health clinics can be particularly helpful to teens with STDs. There are also a variety of national and local support groups that a teen can turn to in time of need. See the Resources section of this book for numbers to call.

REACH OUT TO OTHERS

Teens who accept and come to terms with the fact that they are living with a chronic STD may want to help others learn about prevention and control. There are a variety of ways that teens can become involved, both at school and in the community:

- In health classes, ensure that the most up-to-date information on STDs is presented. Give a report on the subject, get permission to create a bulletin board, or line up a special speaker.
- Work with school administrators and parents' groups to ensure that students are aware of information that is available about STD prevention. For instance, help counselors send for pamphlets and brochures to give to interested students. Help schedule a speaker who will come to the school and give a presentation at an assembly. Teens need to be aware that school administrators have to work within state sex education guidelines when presenting information on STDs.
- Write an editorial or article for a local newspaper about STDs.
- Work with health-care groups in the community. There may be a teen clinic or teen hot line that needs volunteers. It may be necessary to get special training to become a member of such a team.

MIGUEL AND LARISSA

Miguel's doctor advised him to inform all his partners that he has genital warts, but Miguel still lacked the courage to tell Larissa. "Every time I was with her, I was worrying that she was going to get infected," he admits. "When the phone rang, I expected her to be on the other end, yelling that I'd given her warts. I wanted to tell her, but my throat kind of closed up when I thought about it."

Miguel finally remembered that the clinic he visited offered counseling services, so he made another appointment and confided his problem to a nurse there. She was able to give him some suggestions for making the discussion with Larissa a little easier. "I know it's not going to be easy," he says, "but I'm going to tell her. Even if she dumps me, I know I'll have done the right thing."

HOW DO I TELL MY PARTNER?

Telling a partner—especially a new partner—about a chronic STD infection can be an extremely difficult task. Many teens are tempted to keep their secret indefinitely, but that is not a wise idea. Even the most understanding partners are less likely to be accepting of an STD if they discover that they are newly infected.

Teens can minimize discomfort and embarrassment when breaking the news by thinking through what needs to be said, and how, when, and where to say it. Some teens decide to practice by telling a close friend whom they know is accepting, to see what that person's reaction to the news might be.

There are other general guidelines that can help make the discussion a little easier. They include:

- If this is just the beginning of a relationship, get to know a partner first. It is not necessary to reveal that you have an STD on the first date, although you must tell your partner before becoming intimate. If you are already in a sexual relationship, you must tell your partner as soon as possible.

- Pick a private place to talk, where you will not be disturbed or overheard. Pick a place where you are comfortable, preferably not your partner's home. Your home, a park, or the beach are a few possibilities. Talk face-to-face if possible. It's sometimes hard to pick up nuances or gauge a person's body language in a telephone conversation. Some good opening lines could be: "I think I can trust you, so I'd like to tell you something very personal," or "I need to let you know something about me. It may or may not be a big deal to you."

- Don't have your discussion while under the influence of alcohol or drugs.

- Don't start your discussion as you are beginning to have sex or immediately after having sex.

- Have a calm, matter-of-fact approach. The more positive you are, the more likely it will be that your partner will be calm and positive, too. (Try not to use words like "incurable disease," "terrible problem," or "abnormal.") Be open and honest and answer all questions. Convey to your partner that you know a lot about your STD and how to deal with it.

- Give your partner time to adjust. Remember how you felt when you found out you were infected. Don't force a reaction or decision immediately. Avoid becoming angry or judgmental. Treat your partner the way you would like to be treated in the same situation.

- If your partner is accepting of your news, talk about the options—abstinence or safer sex. Be sure to explain how your STD can be spread, so your partner will understand the risk and can take necessary precautions.

There are some people who, for a variety of reasons, cannot handle the risk posed by a partner infected with an STD. A broken relationship can be the result. Everyone faces rejection when it comes to love and relationships, however, even if an STD is not involved. There are also many people who will be understanding and accepting. How a partner responds to the news of an STD can reveal a great deal about his or her principles, values, and character.

WHAT IF I WANT TO HAVE CHILDREN?

People who are infected with genital herpes, genital warts, and HIV/AIDS can still have children. They must exercise precautions to ensure that they do not pass their infection on to their children, however. Before becoming pregnant, it is always wise to check with a doctor. Certain medications that are used to control symptoms of STDs can be dangerous for a developing fetus. Changes in treatment may need to be made while an infected woman is pregnant and nursing.

Proper treatment can dramatically reduce the risk of passing HIV infection from mother to baby during pregnancy, and antiviral medication can prevent an outbreak of herpes that may infect a baby at birth. If a woman is having a herpes outbreak when she is ready to give birth, her doctor may opt to perform a cesarean section—delivering the baby through an incision in the mother's abdomen and uterus—to protect the baby from becoming infected as it passes through the birth canal.

BE SMART AND RESPONSIBLE

Teens today live in risky times when it comes to sex and sexual relations. Yet the times look promising, as well. Researchers, doctors, and public-health officials are working hard to stem the spread of STDs, and in many cases the numbers are decreasing. Teens are getting the message and are choosing to be more responsible when it comes to sexual relationships. Some of them like Nakeesha, Celeste, Nathan, and Miguel have learned the hard way by contracting an STD. Some know friends or family who have had an STD. Some have known people who have died of AIDS.

Whatever a person's prior experience, it is never too late to change one's behavior, to protect oneself from STDs, to get to the doctor and get tested. The most dangerous thing of all is to ignore the facts. In the words of former basketball great Magic Johnson, who was diagnosed with HIV in 1991: "Be smart and be responsible. If you choose abstinence, you're making the safest choice. You're being your own person, and wonderful opportunities for the loving, caring relationship you want still lie ahead untouched by past experience. If you choose to have sex, then please, choose safer sex each and every time."

GLOSSARY

abstinence—doing without something, for example alcohol or sexual relations

antibody—a protein produced by the immune system to fight off infection

antigen—a protein, chemical, or bacteria on the surface of an organism that stimulates the production of antibodies

anus—the opening at the lower end of the large intestine through which waste is released

autoinoculation—an infection caused by a disease that has spread from another part of the body

carrier—an infected person who may be symptom free but who can pass infection to others

cervix—the neck of the uterus, a narrow passage leading to the vagina

chancre—a painless, highly infectious ulcer that is the leading symptom of primary syphilis

clitoris—the small external female sex organ

colposcopy—a procedure by which the vagina is examined using a colposcope, a magnifying and photographic instrument

dissemination—the process of spreading over or through a large area

ectopic pregnancy—the implantation and development of a fertilized egg outside of the uterus

enzyme-linked immunosorbent assay (ELISA)—a diagnostic test in which antigens or antibodies are detected by an enzyme that converts a colorless substance into a colored product

epidemic—an outbreak of disease that spreads more widely or more quickly among a group of people than would normally be expected

epididymis—a convoluted tubule, lying on the testicle, through which sperm pass from the testicle to the vas deferens

fallopian tubes—two narrow tubes through which eggs pass from the ovaries to the uterus

fetus—an unborn human offspring after eight weeks of development

genitals—reproductive organs

human immunodeficiency virus (HIV)—the virus that causes AIDS

human papillomaviruses (HPV)—a large family of viruses that cause warts including genital warts

immune system—a complex body system that aids the body in fighting off disease

immunity—a condition of being protected from disease

infertile—unable to reproduce

intravenous—administered into a vein

labia—fleshy folds that surround the opening of the vagina

lesion—any kind of abnormality of any tissue or organ due to any disease or injury

lymphocytes—a variety of white blood cells consisting of T cells and B cells, both of which are vital to the function of the immune system

monogamous—having a sexual relationship with only one partner during a period of time

neurosyphilis—an infection of the nervous system by *T. pallidum*, the bacterium that causes syphilis

non-nucleoside reverse transcriptase inhibitors (NNRTIs)—a class of HIV-suppressive drugs that block transcription of genetic material inside the virus

nucleoside analogues—a class of HIV-suppressive drugs that work to keep T cells from making more virus

opportunistic infections—conditions caused by microorganisms that may not normally cause disease, but that become life threatening when a host's immunity is impaired

ovary—the female reproductive organ that produces eggs and hormones

Pap smear—a test to detect precancerous or cancerous condition of the cervix

pathogen—an agent such as a bacterium or fungus that causes disease

pelvic inflammatory disease (PID)—an infection of the upper female reproductive tract that can lead to infertility

penis—the male reproductive organ that is used to transfer sperm to the female during sexual intercourse

polymerase chain reaction (PCR)—the technique by which a small fragment of genetic material can be rapidly duplicated to produce multiple copies

prodrome—the period of time immediately prior to an outbreak of herpes; symptoms such as itching, burning, or tingling of the skin can occur during prodrome

prostate—the male reproductive gland lying below the bladder that produces part of the fluid in semen

protease inhibitors—a class of powerful HIV-suppressive drugs that slow the virus's reproduction process

retrovirus—a family of viruses characterized by a unique mode of replication

scrotum—the loose sac of skin and muscles that holds the testicles

semen—a thick white fluid, containing sperm, which is released from the penis during sexual intercourse

seminal vesicle—the male reproductive gland that produces semen

shedding—a condition in which the herpes virus is present on the skin and can be easily passed to others; symptoms of infection may or may not be present

sperm—male reproductive cells, produced in the testicles

syndrome—the symptomatic phase of a herpes infection

testicle—the male reproductive organ that produces sperm and the hormone testosterone

ulcer—a slow-healing sore

urethra—the tube that carries urine (and in the male, semen) out of the body

uterus—the muscular female reproductive organ in the lower abdomen in which a baby develops before birth

vagina—the muscular tube running from the uterus out of the body; the birth canal

vas deferens—the duct through which sperm is carried from the epididymis to the urethra

vulva—external female sex organs including the clitoris, vaginal opening, and labia

Western blot immunoassay—a diagnostic test that looks for antibodies to infectious agents such as herpes and HIV

yeast infection—an infection by a fungus in the vagina, mouth, or other parts of the body, causing irritation and/or other symptoms

RESOURCES

Information about sexually transmitted diseases can be found through a search of the Internet using the key words "Sexually Transmitted Diseases," "STDs," or the specific name of a disease such as "chlamydia" or "genital herpes." Information can also be obtained by calling or writing the following organizations:

American Academy of Pediatrics (AAP)
141 Northwest Point Boulevard
Elk Grove Village, IL 60007-1098
(847) 434-4000
www.aap.org

The AAP's mission is "to attain optimal physical, mental, and social health and well-being for all infants, children, adolescents, and young adults." The organization funds and carries out research and works with the government to ensure that children's health needs are considered when legislation and public policy are developed. Its many publications include manuals on infectious diseases and school health, education brochures, *Healthy Kids* magazine, and a series of child-care books written by AAP members.

American Social Health Association (ASHA)
P.O. Box 13827
Research Triangle Park, NC 27709
(800) 230-6039
www.ashastd.org
www.iwannaknow.org

ASHA's aim is to lessen the harmful consequences of STDs on individuals, families, and communities. The organization's Web site provides information on STDs, support groups, and hot lines. The "I Wanna Know" Web site is specially designed for teens to learn about STDs and sexual health. ASHA publishes *The Helper*, a newsletter about herpes, and *HPV News*, a publication focusing on human papillomavirus.

Centers for Disease Control and Prevention (CDC)
National Center for HIV, STD, and TB Prevention (NCHSTP)
1600 Clifton Road
Atlanta, GA 30333
(800) 311-3435
National STD Hot Line—(800) 227-8922
National AIDS Hot Line—(800) 342-2437
www.cdc.gov/nchstp/dstd/dstdp.html

The NCHSTP is a leader in preventing the spread of HIV, tuberculosis, and STDs. It carries out research and policy development and assists health departments and other health-care providers to meet community needs. The Web site provides information on statistics and trends, research, treatment, and links to related sites. The hot lines offer anonymous, confidential information about STDs and how to prevent them. They also provide referrals to clinics and other services.

CDC National Prevention Information Network (NPIN)
P.O. Box 6003
Rockville, MD 20849-6003
(800) 458-5231
www.cdcnpin.org

NPIN is a national referral, reference, and distribution service sponsored by the CDC. It provides general information about clinics and support groups, answers frequently asked questions, and provides links to other sites. Its education database offers a variety of materials including pamphlets, books, videotapes, posters, and teaching guides.

Free Teens USA
P.O. Box 97
Westwood, NJ 07675
E-mail: FreeTeens@aol.com
www.freeteens.org

Free Teens is an abstinence-centered HIV/AIDS, STDs, and pregnancy prevention program used in many states and countries throughout the world. A variety of publications are available through its Web site, and the *Free Teens* newsletter is published three times a year.

Hepatitis Foundation International (HFI)
30 Sunrise Terrace
Cedar Grove, NJ 07009-1423
(800) 891-0707
www.hepfi.org

HFI focuses on bringing viral hepatitis under control, supporting research, and educating the public and health-care workers about prevention, diagnosis, and treatment. The foundation has a phone support network, the Patient Advocacy/Information Telecommunication System (PATS).

National Institute of Allergy and Infectious Diseases (NIAID)
Office of Communications and Public Liaison
Building 31, Room 7A-50
31 Center Drive MSC 2520
Bethesda, MD 20892-2520
(301) 496-5717
www.niaid.nih.gov

NIAID is part of the National Institutes of Health (NIH), an agency of the U.S. Department of Health and Human Services. NIAID supports biomedical research to prevent, diagnose, and treat illnesses such as AIDS, tuberculosis, and malaria. Its Web site provides an overview of the immune system, as well as information on vaccine development. Material on experimental treatments can be found under the heading Clinical Trials Database.

Planned Parenthood Federation of America
810 Seventh Avenue
New York, NY 10019
(800) 230-PLAN
www.plannedparenthood.org
The organization provides information about STDs, as well as referrals to local clinics across the United States.

FOR FURTHER READING

For Teens

Blake, Jeanne. *Risky Times: How to Be AIDS Smart and Stay Healthy*. New York: Workman Publishing, 1990.

Brodman, Michael. *Straight Talk About Sexually Transmitted Diseases*. New York: Facts On File, 1993.

Ford, Michael Thomas. *100 Questions and Answers About AIDS: A Guide for Young People*. New York: New Discovery Books, 1992.

Kelly, Pat. *Coping When You or a Friend Is HIV-Positive*. Center City, MN: Hazelden Information Education, 1997.

Landau, Elaine. *Sexually Transmitted Diseases*. Springfield, NJ: Enslow Publishers, 1986.

Nourse, Alan E. *Sexually Transmitted Diseases*. New York: Franklin Watts, 1992.

Woods, Samuel G. *Everything You Need to Know About STD: Sexually Transmitted Disease*. New York: The Rosen Publishing Group, 1997.

For Adults

Daugirdas, John T. *STD: Sexually Transmitted Diseases Including HIV/AIDS*. Hinsdale, IL: Medtext, Inc., 1992.

Marr, Lisa. *Sexually Transmitted Diseases: A Physician Tells You What You Need to Know*. Baltimore: The Johns Hopkins University Press, 1998.

Nevid, Jeffrey S. *Choices: Sex in the Age of STDs*. Boston: Allyn & Bacon, 1998.

Reitano, Michael V. *Sexual Health: Questions You Have, Answers You Need*. Allentown, PA: People's Medical Society, 1999.

Schoeberlein, Deborah. *EveryBody: Preventing HIV and Other Sexually Transmitted Diseases Among Teens*. Carbondale, CO: RAD Educational Programs, 2000.

INDEX

125

incidence of, 31
symptoms of, 32–33
transmission of, 31–32
treatment for, 34–35
Chlamydia trachomatis, 31
Ciprofloxacin, 41
Cirrhosis, 83
Clap (*see* Gonorrhea)
Clitoris, 24, 25
Cold sores, 49
Colposcopy, 79
Condoms, 11, 19, 20, 26, 88–90, 92, 93, 102
Congenital syphilis, 42, 44
Conjunctivitis, 32, 33
Corticosteroid creams, 59
Cryotherapy, 80

Delavirdine, 71
Denial, 21
Didanosine, 71
Disseminated gonococcal infection (DGI), 40
Dissemination, 51
Donovanosis, 15
Doxycycline, 35
Drug use, 21, 26, 65

Ectopic pregnancy, 33
Efavirenz, 71
Ejaculation, 22
Electrocautery, 80
Endocarditis, 41
Enzyme-linked immunosorbent assay (ELISA), 34, 56, 69, 70
Epidemics, 14
Epididymis, 22, 23
Erythromycin, 35
Ethnic taboos, 17

Fallopian tubes, 24, 25
Famiciclovir, 57
Female condoms, 90, 102
Female reproductive system, 24–25
Fitz-Hugh-Curtis syndrome, 40
Fluorescent treponemal anti-

body-absorption (FTA-ABS) test, 45
Food and Drug Administration (FDA), 56, 90
Free Teens USA, 119–120

Galen, 14
Genital herpes, 46, 47–60
diagnosis of, 55–56
emotional side effects of, 54–55
incidence of, 49
symptoms of, 51–54
transmission of, 50–51
treatment for, 56–59
Genital warts, 12, 74–80, 102
incidence of, 75–76
treatment of, 79–80
Gonorrhea, 11, 14–15
complications from, 39–40
diagnosis of, 40–41
incidence of, 37–38
transmission of, 38–39
treatment for, 41
Gram's stain test, 40

Hepatitis A, 80–81
Hepatitis B, 73, 80–81
diagnosis of, 84
incidence of, 83
symptoms of, 82–84
transmission of, 81–82
treatment for, 84–85
vaccine for, 85–86, 93
Hepatitis C, 81
Hepatitis D, 84, 85
Hepatitis Foundation International (HFI), 120
Hitchcock, Penny, 73
HIV/AIDS, 12, 21, 47, 50, 53, 59–73
diagnosis of, 69–70
incidence of, 64
symptoms of, 66–68
testing for, 68–69
transmission of, 64–66